T0167758

Inequality and Economic Policy

Essays in Memory of Gary Becker

HOOVER INSTITUTION
STANFORD UNIVERSITY

*The Hoover Institution gratefully acknowledges
the following individuals and foundations
for their significant support of the*
Working Group on Economic Policy
and this publication:

Lynde and Harry Bradley Foundation

Preston and Carolyn Butcher

Stephen and Sarah Page Herrick

Michael and Rosalind Keiser

Koret Foundation

William E. Simon Foundation

John A. Gunn and Cynthia Fry Gunn

Inequality and Economic Policy

Essays in Memory of Gary Becker

EDITED BY
Tom Church
Chris Miller
John B. Taylor

CONTRIBUTING AUTHORS
John H. Cochrane
Charles I. Jones
Edward P. Lazear
Casey B. Mulligan
Kevin M. Murphy
Lee E. Ohanian
James Piereson
Joshua D. Rauh
Emmanuel Saez
George P. Shultz
Jörg L. Spenkuch

HOOVER INSTITUTION PRESS
STANFORD UNIVERSITY   STANFORD, CALIFORNIA

www.hoover.org

Hoover Institution Press Publication No. 664
Hoover Institution at Leland Stanford Junior University,
Stanford, California 94305-6003

First printing 2015
22 21 20 19 18 17 16 15   9 8 7 6 5 4 3 2 1

Manufactured in the United States of America

The paper used in this publication meets the minimum requirements of the American National Standard for Information Sciences—Permanence of Paper for Printed Library Materials, ANSI/NISO z39.48-1992.⊚

Cataloging-in-Publication Data is available from the Library of Congress.
ISBN-13: 978-0-8179-1904-7 (cloth : alk. paper)
ISBN-13: 978-0-8179-1906-1 (epub)
ISBN-13: 978-0-8179-1907-8 (mobi)
ISBN-13: 978-0-8179-1908-5 (PDF)

In Memoriam

*This conference volume is dedicated to
the life and work of Gary Becker.*

Contents

List of Tables and Figures

Tables

Figures

Acknowledgments

We are grateful to many people for their help in putting together both the conference and this conference volume, including Barbara Arellano, Marshall Blanchard, Nick Brady, Tess Evans Clark, John Cogan, Barbara Egbert, Denise Elson, Scott Harrison, Linda Hernandez, Stephen Langlois, Guity Nashat, Jennifer Navarrette, John Raisian, Marie-Christine Slakey, Janet Smith, and Ian Wright.

Introduction

Tom Church, Chris Miller, and John B. Taylor

The inspiration for these essays is the life and career of Gary Becker. One of the leading economists of his generation and a winner of the Nobel Prize, Becker was a senior fellow at the Hoover Institution for over twenty years. Importantly for the purposes of these essays, Becker was also a leading researcher on the subjects of human capital and income inequality. Many of the questions raised by Becker's research continue to spark vigorous debate among economists, none more so than the effect of inequalities of human capital. The diverse ways in which the essays bring data and analysis to bear on the questions of human capital and inequality are a fitting demonstration of Gary Becker's lasting influence on economics.

The question of income inequality has risen to the forefront of public debate in recent years. Has income inequality increased? If so, what factors are driving this shift? What is the relationship between inequality of income, wealth, and consumption? Is there persistence of inequality from one generation to another? To what extent should we consider higher income inequality a problem? And what role, if any, should public policy play in addressing it?

In different ways, economists have always been interested in, and have debated, these questions. Yet while the essays in this volume engage with these long-term debates, they are motivated by two recent developments. The first is increased interest in inequality, both among the public at large and within the political process.

If we are going to talk about inequality, we need a solid factual and theoretical basis underlying our discussions. All of the essays presented here are written in part with this goal in mind. A second motivation for the essays is the exceptional array of new empirical work on inequality, especially on the incomes and wealth of top earners. Understanding these new data requires careful study and interpretation, and these essays all aim to address this issue.

For Gary Becker, economics and economic policy were inseparable. When he talked to a politician running for office or to a public official already in office, his policy recommendations would be exactly the same as if he were speaking to a student or a colleague. Gary Becker was diagnosing and looking for solutions to income distribution problems decades ago. And some of his most recent work at the Hoover Institution was on inequality across generations.

In chapter 1, James Piereson outlines the existing debate on inequality, surveying the data collected by Thomas Piketty and Emmanuel Saez that show a remarkable increase in top incomes. From a public policy perspective, Piereson argues, inequality presents a serious intellectual challenge, because many policies that could reduce inequality might also slow economic growth.

Joshua Rauh asks, in chapter 2, why top incomes have increased rapidly in recent decades. Drawing on a wide array of data, Rauh shows that top incomes have increased across different sectors, from corporate managers to sports stars. Rauh concludes that this suggests broad market forces such as globalization or technological change caused top incomes to rise.

In chapter 3, Chad Jones proposes a model to explain why inequality varies across different countries. He examines how the processes of creative destruction and innovation interact to shape the returns to entrepreneurship. Jones's model suggests that a wide range of variables—from research subsidies to barriers to market entry—affect inequality levels.

Jorg Spenkuch develops a model of an equally important issue in chapter 4, exploring the relationship between intergenerational mobility and income inequality. Spenkuch argues that parents with high human capital are likely to invest more effectively in the development of human capital in their children. Spenkuch argues that this fact explains why children of parents at the top of the income distribution are themselves likely to reach the top of the income distribution. Another surprising conclusion is that increasing education spending by an equal amount per student might lead to an increase in inequality.

In chapter 5, Casey Mulligan explores the downsides to policies which are often used to combat inequality. Mulligan shows how policies such as changes to health insurance and anti-poverty programs raise implicit tax rates on employment. Arguing that higher taxes on employment in recent years have caused lower employment levels, Mulligan cautions against ignoring the side effects of policies intended to reduce inequality.

Emmanuel Saez and Kevin Murphy debate the causes of rising top incomes in chapter 6. Murphy focuses on human capital, arguing that high demand and low supply of highly educated workers have pushed up top wages. Helping lower-skilled workers increase their human capital, he suggests, would reduce inequality while promoting economic growth. By contrast, Saez suggests that rent-seeking explains much of the increase in top incomes and argues that government needs to play a big role in reducing inequality.

In chapter 7, John Cochrane, Lee Ohanian, and George Shultz examine the implications for public policy. Cochrane argues that inequality is an unhelpful intellectual framework and suggests that focusing on inequality distracts from challenges such as promoting economic growth and decreasing poverty. Ohanian argues that improved education and increased immigration could boost wages for low-income workers. George Shultz concludes by discussing two case studies of organizations that work to fight poverty and related social ills.

In the final chapter, Eddie Lazear and George Shultz reminisce about the life and career of Gary Becker. Becker's work touched a wide range of subjects, from the economics of sports to family structures. Lazear and Shultz celebrate Becker's path-breaking research and share personal stories borne out of decades of friendship.

Together, the chapters illustrate the complexity of scholarly debate about income inequality. Not only do economists disagree about which forces are driving changes in the distribution of income, they also continue to debate the relevance of inequality itself as a concept for public discussion and policymaking. Needless to say, given the complexity of the issue, income inequality is a topic that economists will be debating for some time to come. The essays presented here, however, not only represent the current state of economic thinking regarding inequality, they lay out a rich agenda for future research. In that sense, these essays not only constitute a remembrance of Gary Becker, but also a continuation of his scholarly work.

CHAPTER ONE

Background Facts

James Piereson

Our subject is the inequality crisis, so called. I somewhat regret the title of my book, *The Inequality Hoax.* If you've published anything lately, you know that your publishers want an attention-drawing title on your book or article. I could not call the book "The Inequality Dilemma" or "The Inequality Challenge"; those titles are too equivocal. That's more or less what it is: a challenge or a dilemma, and one that will be difficult to address. My view is that inequality is real, however you want to measure it. But the subject is being used in ways that are not helpful and could do a great deal of harm if we're not careful. I'll elaborate on that view.

We've experienced a series of crises over our lifetimes. I think back to the poverty crisis of the 1960s, the urban crisis of the 1960s, the energy crisis of the 1970s, the inflation crisis, later the homeless crisis, the health care crisis, and the global warming crisis today. Many people find it helpful politically to talk in terms of crisis, perhaps as a way of stampeding voters into doing things they might not otherwise do. If we look back over these crises, it's not clear that we've responded to them in ways that have always been helpful.

Today we have what some have called "the new inequality." The old inequality was all about helping the poor move up into the middle class: think about the poverty programs in the 1960s or

I want to acknowledge the invaluable assistance of Carson Bruno in the preparation of this paper.

spending on education. Federal programs of all sorts were designed to allow the poor to rise. The inequality crisis today is from the other end. It's about the top 1 percent of the income distribution, and finding ways to redistribute that income down through the population to raise the living standards of the other 99 percent. We've been talking about this for a number of years, but it surged into public consciousness last spring with the publication of Thomas Piketty's book, *Capital in the Twenty-First Century*. It was a monumental bestseller, and was widely read and reviewed. Piketty became an overnight celebrity. It is a carefully researched and closely argued book. I encourage everybody to read it. It's an impressive work. It's very insightful in a lot of ways and it makes a case that puts inequality in a historical and intellectual context. In a certain sense, he's done for inequality what Marx did for capitalism. In the nineteenth century, intellectuals and radicals complained about the factory system, the movement of people into the cities, the exploitation of labor, and other developments associated with the rise of industry. But it was Marx who placed it into a theoretical and historical context.

In the 1920s and 1930s, many people were talking about public spending and public works as a way to deal with unemployment. It was John Maynard Keynes who put that into a broader theoretical context to explain how public spending could be used to manipulate or jumpstart the economy during the Depression. In a certain sense, Piketty (along with his colleague, Emmanuel Saez) has done something similar for inequality. They've placed it into a broad intellectual context. It's the strongest statement we have of what we might call "the redistributionist thesis." They have done an impressive job of collecting a great deal of data on wealth and income extending back into the 1800s in the case of a few countries. With respect to the United States, they have collected data on wealth and income going back to 1900. These data are not perfect in every respect. The wealth data in particular were arrived at via some sophisticated statistical estimation. Governments collect income data because they tax income. They don't collect data on wealth. For this reason, Piketty and his associates had to piece together the data on wealth using estimation techniques from estate tax filings. People have criticized their data. I do not, because I expect that they will improve the data over time. In addition, no one else, to this point, has done a better job.

Piketty makes the theoretical case that inequality is built into the fabric of the capitalist order. It's not accidental but fundamental: inequality will inevitably explode unless it is counteracted by active governmental measures. Their remedy to redistribute income is not complex; they call for a return to the high and confiscatory tax rates on the wealthy that were in place in most countries from the 1930s into the 1970s.

The basic theory is that returns to capital always grow more quickly than output in the economy or returns to labor. If that pattern persists over time, then those who own capital grow wealthier over time. In Figure 1.1, taken from Piketty's *Capital in the 21st Century*, one sees that in the middle of the twentieth century returns to capital declined and were overtaken by overall economic output. For that reason, there was a rough equalization of incomes during that period. Later in the century, after about 1980, inequality increased because capital accumulated faster than the output of the world economy.

What we conclude from this is that the modern age of capitalism can be divided up into three periods. The first period, running from roughly 1870 to 1929 in the United States and from 1870 to 1914 in Europe, was the original gilded age of inequality. The middle period, running roughly from 1930 to 1980, might be called the "golden age of social democracy," marked by high marginal tax rates, output growing more rapidly than returns to capital, and

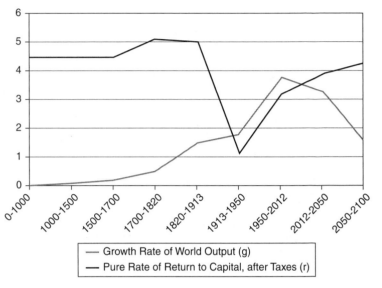

FIGURE 1.1. Rate of return vs. world growth (antiquity to 2100)
Source: Thomas Piketty, *Capital in the 21st Century,* figure 10.10, p. 356

a greater equalization of incomes and wealth. Beginning in 1980 and moving forward to the present time, we have lived through a new gilded age of rising inequality and returns to growth going disproportionately to the wealthy. That is the tripartite division of the history of modern capitalism, which I more or less accept on the basis of the data marshaled by Piketty and his associates.

Figure 1.2 displays a set of data on after-tax income from the Congressional Budget Office. The data cover the period from 1979 to 2010. The top dotted line displays the percentage growth in income from year to year for the top 1 percent of the income distribution; the bottom line displays the same variable for the bottom 99 percent. The line displays the evolution of the median income for the entire population, which tracks closely with the incomes of the bottom 99 percent of the distribution. The basic problem is that the income of the top 1 percent is exploding and the income for the rest is increasing much more slowly, though (importantly)

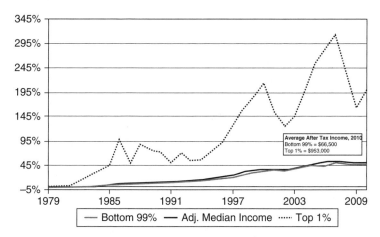

FIGURE 1.2. Average after-tax income growth (1979 to 2010)

Source: Travis Honeyfield, ed., "Distribution of Household Income & Federal Taxes, 2008–2010," tables 3 & 5 (Washington, DC: Congressional Budget Office)

it is not declining. The mean after-tax income for the top 1 percent in 2010 was $953,000 and for the bottom 99 it was $66,000. The figures are for after-tax income; the distribution of pre-tax income is slightly more skewed in favor of the wealthy, as there is a mildly redistributive element to the federal tax system.

Placing these figures within a longer historical frame, it is apparent that the great increase in inequality since 1980 represented a departure from the pattern of earlier decades. Figure 1.3, taken from an article by Saez, displays the share of pre-tax income (with and without capital gains) received by the top 1 percent and 0.1 percent in the United States between 1913 and 2010. The data begin in 1913 because that is the year the United States launched the income tax. The lines follow a recognizable U-shaped pattern, with the wealthy reaping higher shares of national income before 1930, then somewhat smaller shares between 1930 and 1980, and once again much higher shares during the three-decade period after 1980. Today the top 1 percent of the income distribution is receiving close to 20 percent of national income, a figure close to what it

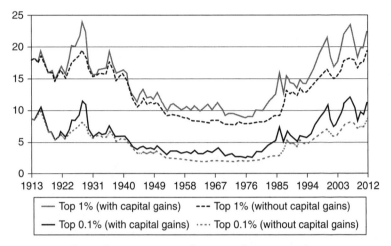

FIGURE 1.3. Share of pre-tax, pre-transfer income for top 1% and 0.1%

Source: Emmanuel Saez, "Income Inequality in the United States, 1913–1998," with Thomas Piketty, *Quarterly Journal of Economics,* 118(1), 2003, 1–39, updated to 2012, September 2013, tables A1 and A3

was in the 1920s. In the intervening decades—1930 to 1980—those shares dropped by half to around 10 percent of national income. This chart more or less encapsulates Piketty's historical narrative: the original gilded age broken up by the stock market crash of 1929 and the New Deal, the "golden age" of social democracy from 1930 to 1980, and the return of the gilded age in recent decades.

Piketty also points out that the wealthy in our era earn their incomes from different sources than was the case early in the twentieth century. In the early decades of the century, the wealthy received most of their income from capital gains—that is, by earnings from stocks and bonds rather than from salaries and wages. In the parlance of the day, they were "coupon clippers," passively receiving income from investments. In the contemporary era, the wealthy are increasingly professionals who earn generous salaries from executive positions. Today, more than half of the total income of the top 1 percent is received in the form of salaries. These are people who work for a living and depend upon salaries to pay their bills and accumulate wealth.

Piketty focuses a good deal of attention on the so-called "new salaried rich"—those who earn salaries of between $300,000 and $1 million per year as executives in businesses, financial firms, colleges and universities, and not-for-profit organizations. He does not believe that they genuinely earn these salaries on the basis of their contributions to the profitability or efficiency of the organizations they run; rather, he suggests, they set their own salaries, or recruit board members who support generous compensation packages, and in general receive high pay packages as members of a "club" with wealthy associates and directors.

The evidence for these claims is thin and impressionistic. Nevertheless, from his point of view, they justify much higher tax rates on members of the new managerial class, particularly since he believes that the lower marginal tax rates of the post-1980 decades have created a permissive environment for boards of directors that set salaries for executives. In the old days, with a 91 percent marginal tax rate, it did not make a lot of sense for boards to approve overly generous salaries, since most of the added increment went to the federal government in the form of taxes. High marginal tax rates thus tended to keep executive salaries down. Today, the logic is different: with low marginal rates, salaried professionals can keep most of their raises.

As one would expect from these figures, there are now significant differences among different segments of the national economy in mean household incomes and net worth. In 2010, as depicted in table 1.1, the mean household income of the top 1 percent was $1.3 million while the bottom 40 percent received on average about $17,000. The disparities are even greater for household net worth, measured in terms of ownership of real estate and financial assets.

TABLE 1.1. Income and net worth in the US by percentile (2010 dollars, averages)

Wealth or Income Class	Mean Household Income	Mean Household Net Worth	Mean Household Financial (Non-Home) Wealth
Top 1%	$1,318,200	$16,439,400	$15,171,600
80th to 99th%	107,000	1,295,600	1,010,800
60th to 80th%	72,000	216,900	100,700
40th to 60th%	41,700	61,000	12,200
Bottom 40%	17,300	(10,600)	(14,800)

Note: Only mean figures are available, not medians. Note that income and wealth are separate measures; so, for example, the top 1 percent of income-earners is not exactly the same group of people as the top 1 percent of wealth-holders, although there is considerable overlap.

Source: Edward Wolff, "The Asset Price Meltdown and the Wealth of the Middle Class," August 26, 2012, table 4
Data source: Survey on Consumer Finances

It is hard to quibble with Piketty and his associates in their claim that inequalities in wealth and income are substantial and growing decade by decade.

Piketty and Saez argue that these patterns justify aggressive national policies to redistribute income through higher taxes on the wealthy. Though the argument is logical, there are several problems with it.

First, though the very wealthy have gained in terms of shares of income and wealth, they have also been paying a larger share of the income tax in the United States. From 1979–2010, the tax liability on the top 1 percent has increased sharply, even as we have reduced marginal tax rates. In 1979, the highest earners paid federal taxes at a marginal rate of 70 percent. Ronald Reagan (and a Democratic Congress) reduced that rate to 50 percent in 1981 and then later to 28 percent. Nevertheless, the share of federal income taxes paid by the top 20 percent of the income distribution increased from 65 percent in 1979 to 93 percent by 2010. The top 1 percent paid 17 percent of income taxes in 1979 but 37 percent in 2010.

Today, then, the top 20 percent of the income distribution pays nearly the whole of our federal income taxes. As we have reduced marginal rates, we have also taken those below the median income completely off the federal income tax rolls (they are still hit with payroll taxes). This, then, points to one of the difficulties in redistributive taxation: there is not a lot of room to raise taxes on "the rich." They are already paying the lion's share of the income tax. It also points to the political difficulty in trying to cut taxes: any tax cut will disproportionately favor the wealthy because they are the ones already paying the taxes.

Second, it is not at all clear that we can reduce inequality very much through the income tax system. In theory, taxpayers would send money to Washington, DC, and from there the political authorities would allocate it to those who need it for the purpose of equalizing incomes. But that is not the way the political system actually operates. Money sent to Washington must pass through a gantlet of interest groups seeking concentrated benefits for their members. In the struggle for funds, the politically influential groups usually win out over disorganized voters seeking small and widely dispersed benefits. In addition, the immediate beneficiaries of the national tax system appear to be those living in or around the nation's capital. Five of the six wealthiest counties in the United States surround Washington. The capital already has the highest per capita income of any metropolitan region in the country. Under current circumstances, a tax increase on the wealthy would merely redistribute income from the top 1 percent to the next 2 percent or 3 percent of the income distribution.

It is true that there is some "real" money in the top income groups. The top 1 percent paid about $400 billion in federal taxes in 2010, leaving them with about $1.1 trillion in after-tax income. It might be possible to gain another $100 billion to $200 billion by raising their taxes by another 10 percent or 20 percent. That is not a large sum in relation to a federal budget of close to $4 trillion, but it would represent a significant proportion of the current federal deficit of $400 billion to $500 billion. But, for reasons stated above, it is unlikely that those added revenues would eventually end up where Piketty and his colleagues think they should.

An obvious limitation of the income tax is that it does not get at the extraordinary accumulations of wealth held by individuals like Warren Buffett, Bill Gates, and other members of the Forbes 400. Governments tax incomes, but not wealth. The very wealthy own a disproportionate share of these assets. According to some estimates, the wealthiest 1 percent own close to half of the $80 trillion to $90 trillion value of the stock, bond, and residential real estate markets.

As a remedy for this problem, Piketty advocates a global "wealth tax" on the "super-wealthy," with that tax levied against assets in stocks, bonds, and real estate. He acknowledges that such a tax has little chance of being enacted, though he hopes that at some point it might be enacted to cover the countries in the European Union. The United States has never had a wealth tax; and in fact such a tax may not be allowed under the Constitution (which authorizes taxes on incomes). Several European countries—Germany, Finland, and Sweden among them—have had such a tax in the past, but have discontinued it. France currently has a wealth tax that tops out at a rate of 1.5 percent on assets in excess of ten million Euros (or about $14 million).

Wealth taxes are notoriously difficult to collect, and they encourage capital flight, hiding of assets, and disputes over pricing of assets. They require individuals to sell assets to pay taxes, thereby causing asset values to fall. Piketty thinks that a capital tax would have to be global in nature to guard against both capital flight and the hiding of assets in foreign accounts. It would also require a new international banking regime under which major banks would be required to disclose account information to national treasuries. Under his scheme, a tax would be imposed on a sliding scale beginning at 1 percent on modest fortunes (roughly between $1.5 million and $7 million) and perhaps reaching as high as 10 percent on "super fortunes" in excess of $1 billion annually. The purpose of the tax, it should be stressed, is to reduce inequality, not to spend the new revenues on beneficial public purposes.

Professor Piketty argues in the broader message of his book that we are living through a new "gilded age" of extravagant wealth and lavish expenditures enjoyed by a narrow elite at the expense of everyone else. As with the original "gilded age" of the late nineteenth century, the wealth accruing to the few gives the illusion of progress and prosperity, but conceals growing hardships and economic difficulties endured by the rest of the population. Much of his thesis rests upon this proposition: our era is one of faux prosperity, a claim that is manifestly untrue.

This argument makes sense only if one accepts the narrow premise that these multifaceted regimes can be assessed on the basis of the single criterion of wealth and income distribution or that the essence of the capitalist order is found solely in returns to capital and in the distribution of wealth and incomes rather than in rising living standards, innovation, and the spread of modern civilization. In each of these three eras, there was much more going on than simply the rearranging of wealth and incomes.

No less an authority than John Maynard Keynes looked back upon the pre-war era in Europe as a "golden age" of capitalism. "What an extraordinary episode in the economic progress of man that age was which came to an end in August, 1914," he wrote in 1919 in *The Economic Consequences of the Peace*. He marveled at the economic progress made across the continent after 1870 following the unification of Germany. Industry and population grew steadily as trade across the continent accelerated, widening the sphere of prosperity and the reach of modern comforts. In the United States, rapid growth, stable prices, and high real wages drew millions of immigrants from Europe to build railroads, work in factories, and industrialize the country. Far-reaching innovations—electricity, the telegraph, mass-produced steel, and motorcars—drove the industrial process forward and made a few people very rich. It was the first era of globalization and open trade. These three factors— innovation, emigration toward emerging centers of wealth, and widening circles of trade—have been key elements of "golden ages" throughout history, and especially in the modern age of capitalism. This particular golden age ended in 1914 in Europe and in 1929 in the United States.

The so-called "golden age" of social democracy has much to commend it; one should not gainsay the genuine economic and social progress achieved in the United States and elsewhere during the middle decades of the century. Nevertheless, the virtues of that era can be overstated. As Piketty acknowledges, much of the accumulated capital of the preceding era was wiped out by war and depression. The confiscatory tax rates of that era, with marginal rates as high as 91 percent in the United States in the 1940s and 1950s, may have equalized incomes to some degree but they also discouraged effort and held back risk-taking and innovation. The impressive growth rates of the 1950s and 1960s developed from a depressed base and built out innovations from the earlier period. Labor unions grew and won impressive wage gains for members, but mainly because (in the United States) they were bargaining with domestic oligopolies in the auto, steel, railroad, aluminum, and other industries. The structure of American industry was highly concentrated which, in the opinion of some, impeded innovation. Economist John Kenneth Galbraith wrote that cartelization was a permanent feature of the US economy. There was little immigration into the United States and Western Europe between 1930 and 1970. Most importantly for the distribution of wealth, the US stock market barely moved in real terms between 1930 and 1980; in 1980, the Dow Jones Industrial Average was at a lower level (adjusted for inflation) than at its peak in 1929.

The high tax regime of that era collapsed in the 1970s, not because "the rich" dismantled it, but because government spending and regulation brought with them more crime, dependency, and disorder, along with simultaneously growing rates of unemployment and inflation. It was Jimmy Carter who first led the charge to deregulate the airline, railroad, trucking, and communications industries. Democrats and Republicans alike agreed that the US economy was suffering from a shortage of capital—and that tax rates should be reduced to promote capital formation. That approach succeeded, as we have seen. At the same time, US leaders pushed successfully for the elimination of trade barriers and a more open international trading system.

One might echo Keynes's comments about the pre-war era in Europe in reflecting upon the era through which we have lived from the 1980s to the present. This has been, as some have called it, the "age of Reagan"—an era defined by the tax and regulatory reforms he put in place during the 1980s. Far from being a gilded age, it appears from a broader perspective to have been a new golden age of capitalism, marked by life-changing innovations in technology, globalized markets, and widening circles of trade, unprecedented levels of immigration into centers of prosperity, the absence of major wars, rising living standards around the world, falling inflation and interest rates, and a thirty-year bull market in stocks, bonds, and real estate. At the same time, the boom in financial assets and real estate has also enriched the endowments of colleges, universities, and foundations, along with pension and retirement funds upon which millions of households depend.

These developments broke up the concentrated structure of the US economy, making it more open, competitive, and innovative. At the same time, corporate profits are far higher now than in the age of industrial concentration and oligopoly. The end of the Cold War and the entrance of China into the world economy similarly broke open the structure of world politics and finance that dominated the middle decades of the century. Meanwhile, levels of poverty and inequality around the world have declined dramatically over the past three decades. Though some have won incredible riches in this new age of capitalism, they have done so by developing new products and technologies of benefit to everyone, or by investing in enterprises that earn profits by satisfying customers.

Keynes once remarked that the challenge in such a situation is to keep "the boom" going, not to bring it to a premature end out of a superstition that those who have prospered must be punished by high taxes and self-defeating regulations. Those errors have been made in the past, most recently in the 1930s. Our golden age is going to end sooner or later, but much sooner if Professor Piketty and his supporters have their way.

This is because our main challenge is not in the area of inequality but in sustaining the economic growth that is the real solution to stagnating middle-class incomes. Economic growth has

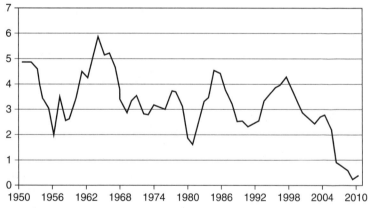

FIGURE 1.4. Annual five-year moving average real GDP growth (%) 1950–2011
Source: Bureau of Economic Activity

been slowing decade by decade in the United States and across the industrial world, and particularly since the year 2000. The stock market boom of recent decades has sustained the wealth and incomes of the top 1 percent, but it has done little for the living standards of the middle and working classes.

This point is illustrated more clearly in figure 1.4, which displays the pattern of real GDP per capita economic growth from 1950 through 2011. The pattern is displayed in five-year moving averages in order to remove the "noise" of year-to-year changes so that the long-term trend can be seen more clearly. As the chart suggests, the US economy has gone through three extended boom periods over the past sixty-plus years: the first in the 1960s, the second in the 1980s, and a third in the 1990s. Yet each recovery has been less robust in GDP growth than its predecessor. In between, the nation has gone through periods of sluggish growth, including an extended one in the 1970s that set the stage for the fairly robust recoveries of the Reagan and Clinton years. From the late 1990s onward, the pattern has been steadily downward, and much more sharply and for much longer than in previous sluggish periods.

The United States may have an inequality problem, but more fundamentally it has a "growth" problem. A stagnant America, lacking growth and broad opportunities for advancement and achievement, would represent something new and dangerous for a nation whose ideals and institutions have been built upon a foundation of growth and prosperity. The emphasis on inequality and redistribution, while not wrong, is nevertheless misplaced, for it may lead us to adopt policies that will disrupt the progress we have made while doing nothing to promote the kind of growth that is essential to national progress.

CHAPTER TWO

The Broad-Based Rise in the Return to Top Talent

Joshua D. Rauh

My talk here today is called, "It's the Market: The Broad-Based Rise in the Return to Top Talent." This is work that I've done with Steve Kaplan. We've been working on this for quite a while now. I think that we first started on it maybe seven or eight years ago. It's an honor to be here and to be presenting this work in memory of Gary Becker, whose ideas clearly pervade everything about which we're talking here today.

What do we know about the top 1 percent? There are some very clear facts. It is well known that the top 1 percent of taxable income represents a much greater share than it did thirty years ago. This is largely a story of market income—that is, of pre-tax and of pre-transfer income. If you look at what tax policy and transfers have done to the after-tax, after-transfer income of the top 1 percent, the changes over the last several decades are a lot more muted. Capital gains and options play a role, but the main drivers appear to be labor income and business income.

To illustrate this point again as an introduction to my remarks, let me show you some graphs. Figure 2.1 shows the share of US income going to the top 1 percent from 1979 to 2011. If you look before taxes and transfers, in 1979, it was 10 percent. In 2011, it was over 20 percent. If you look at numbers from the CBO (Congressional Budget Office), which considers income after accounting for taxes and transfers, there has still been a change over the last thirty years. But the change has been more muted, and there's volatility

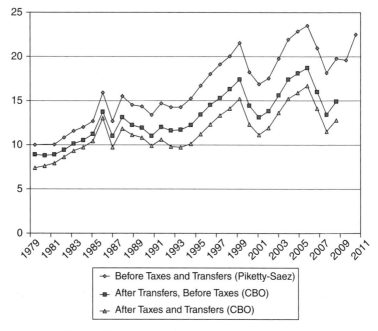

FIGURE 2.1. Share of US income to top 1 percent, 1979–2011

Source: Steven N. Kaplan and Joshua Rauh, "It's the Market: The Broad-Based Rise in the Return to Top Talent," *Journal of Economic Perspectives* 27(3): Summer 2013, 35–56

in the series. If you look at income accounting for tax policy and transfer policy, it'd be hard to say that there's been an explosion in the after-tax/after-transfer income share going to the top 1 percent. It's gone up and down, probably with the market and with the economy, but it's been relatively flat. So, that's one motivating fact.

Another motivating fact is that capital gains play a role. I'm going to talk to you today about some market-related phenomena. As such, some income of the top 1 percent is related to the stock market. But that is not the whole story. Figure 2.2 shows the share going to the top 1 percent, including and excluding capital gains. This is also a graph that we saw earlier today in some form. Capital gains are of course playing a role, but their contribution to top

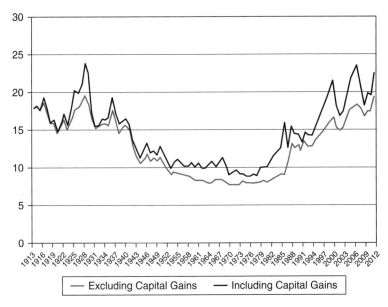

FIGURE 2.2. Capital gains play a role but are not the big story

Source: Emmanuel Saez, "Income Inequality in the United States, 1913–1998," with Thomas Piketty, *Quarterly Journal of Economics,* 118(1), 2003, 1–39, updated to 2012, September 2013

1 percent income inequality has not expanded very much in the past several decades.

Professor Kaplan and I have been trying to better understand the drivers of top 1 percent income inequality by examining what occupations have occupied the top 1 percent both several decades ago and today. We have done this in a series of papers. We've studied the increase in pay in the highest income levels across occupations, as well as changes in the occupations and backgrounds of the wealthiest Americans, to try to get a better sense of what it is that's driving top 1 percent income inequality.

In looking at the literature and at the ideas that are out there about top 1 percent income inequality, one finds two main categories of ideas. The first set of ideas are what I would call the

"It's-the-Market" ideas. There are a number of different variants of this concept. One of the hallmarks of "It's-the-Market" ideas is that there is some kind of interaction between scale and superstar producers, along the lines of the paper by Sherwin Rosen published in the *American Economic Review* in 1981. That paper argues that communications extended the scale on which talent can operate. Rosen was quite prescient writing this paper in 1981, because thanks to technology, the scale on which talent can operate is today much greater than it was in 1981. In the past several decades, we have felt the full impact of the personal computer, personal cell phones, the Internet, and other information technology innovations. The scale-superstar hypothesis is therefore one of the prime examples of the "It's-the-Market" hypothesis. Since the 1980s, that theory has been expanded upon and built upon in a number of different ways.

One of the other key aspects of the "It's-the-Market" hypothesis is the notion that there's been skill-biased technological change. Technology has changed in such a way that it makes the capabilities of the most educated or skilled workers in the economy more valuable. That's a theory that has been very impactful. Other related "It's-the-Market" theories are that you can have small dispersions in talent multiplied by growing organizations, which can lead to growing pay dispersion. This theory was put forth in a paper by Xavier Gabaix and Augustin Landier, published in the *Quarterly Journal of Economics* in 2008. It very much builds upon the scale-superstar theory of Rosen. The idea is that if you have very small differences in talent, scale increases are likely to cause growing pay dispersion. What we then have is an explanation for rising income inequality. The talented are able to multiply their talents across much larger pools of capital or people who they can reach. This talent-multiplication theory is another "It's-the-Market" theory, because increases in income inequality are driven by increasing size of enterprises and scope of talent to generate output. This is an important idea as we honor Gary Becker: the notion that there are increasing returns to the work of individuals with certain types of skills and in particular with a certain type of education, which is an idea related to skill-biased technological change.

The opposing view of rising income inequality is what I would call the "It's the Rents of the Powerful and Wealthy." That is the idea that executives, who are top earners in the economy, are essentially setting their own pay. The argument is that CEOs of publicly traded companies can set their own pay because they control boards of directors. In so doing they can expropriate shareholders and other stakeholders. Related to that, there may have been a breakdown of social norms against high pay levels. Jim Piereson outlined the argument that there has been an interaction between taxes and the returns to rent-seeking. If marginal tax rates are low, then the returns to rent-seeking would be higher. Lower tax rates would then provide higher-powered incentives to engage in rent-seeking, which would then tend to increase the earnings of the top 1 percent. Some of these "Rents-of-the-Powerful-and-Wealthy" ideas have recently received a lot of attention in the book of Thomas Piketty, *Capital in the Twenty-First Century.*

In our research, Professor Steven Kaplan and I look at patterns in occupations of the top 1 percent of earners in the economy, and also at individuals who are at the top of the distribution of wealth in the economy. We ask the question: what do the data on the identity of the top earners in the economy imply about theories of income inequality? Do they favor the "It's-the-Market" theories, or do they favor the "Rents-of-the-Powerful-and-Wealthy" theories?

The first category at which we look is CEOs of publicly traded companies. There are two ways to look at CEO pay. One is that you can look at it based on the grant date or ex-ante pay. Ex-ante pay is the compensation that boards are giving CEOs in a financial value sense when granted, equal to salary + bonus + restricted stock + the value of options when they are granted. Some think of the value of options when they are granted as a sort of expected value of their ultimate worth, although I should emphasize that is not the expected value exactly, but rather the market value of options using a Black-Scholes pricing formula. The ex-ante measure is the most relevant measure for evaluating what boards actually believe they are paying.

Another way to look at CEO pay is through looking at realized pay—in other words, what CEOs actually get. That would be salary + bonus + restricted stock + the value of options exercised or realized. That may be more relevant for evaluating pay for performance because, in this calculation, the options are viewed as being received, and they are valued at the point when they're actually exercised. It's an ex-post measure.

So what has happened to average CEO pay in the United States for publicly traded companies since 2000? Has it gone up? Is it flat? Or has it decreased?

One of the things that inspired us to do this research in the first place was that there seemed to be a generally pervasive notion in the US that average CEO pay has been spinning out of control. This was related to the narrative of CEOs expropriating shareholders or other stakeholders. And indeed, I think that many of you might have heard the popular narrative and believed that CEO pay has gone up. We decided to look at the data.

Figure 2.3 shows what happened. If you look at CEO pay, there was a big increase in the late 1990s, a lot of it related to the value of stock options granted to technology companies. Since 2000, there has not been much change. The graph shows the ex-ante CEO pay, in inflation-adjusted millions of 2012 dollars. These are S&P 500 CEOs. You can see what the average and median pay is for S&P 500 over this time period. The median pay for CEOs is today about the same as it was in 2000. The average, which of course is

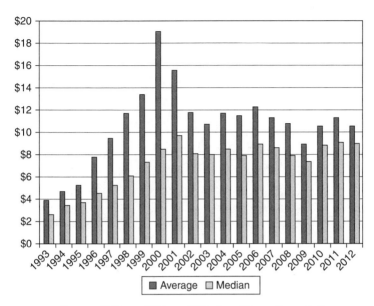

FIGURE 2.3. Ex-ante CEO pay, S&P 500 CEOs in millions of 2012 dollars

Source: ExecuComp and Compustat Index Constituent File, calculations by Steven N. Kaplan and Joshua Rauh

going to be skewed by outliers on the far-right tail, has gone down since that time period. Right now, pay for CEOs looks about the same as it was in the late 1990s.

CEOs in publicly traded companies get a lot of attention. One of the reasons is that the data on what CEOs are paid is easily available from 10-K forms and from disclosures from publicly traded companies. Observers can open the 10-K online and see that the CEO made a hundred times what the average worker in his firm did. But if you look at how CEO pay has changed over time, it has been really quite flat.

In figure 2.4, we look at realized pay. Realized pay is going to be more volatile, and it's going to vary more with the stock market. Of course, CEOs are going to exercise more options when the market

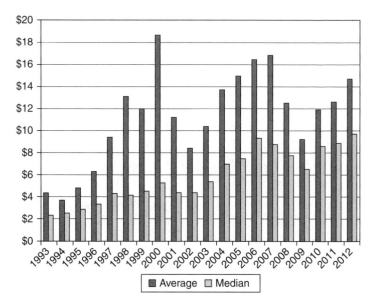

FIGURE 2.4. Realized CEO pay, S&P 500 CEOs in millions of 2012 dollars

Source: ExecuComp and Compustat Index Constituent File, calculations by Steven N. Kaplan and Joshua Rauh

is high. Here things have been more volatile but, again, you don't see an explosion in CEO pay, although median realized CEO pay has increased with the stock market.

Another interesting way to look at CEO pay is relative to the net income of the firm. This has been an area of focus. In figure 2.5, we plot what percentage of the total net income of the S&P 500 is being paid out to the CEO of the firm. CEO pay in 2012 as a fraction of net income looks pretty low relative to the 1990s. The level of CEO pay in 2012 as a share of net income is between 0.5 percent and 1.0 percent, depending on whether we are using ex-ante pay or realized pay including the value of options exercised. This compares to levels of 1.0–1.5 percent in 1997–1999 and 1.5–2.0 percent in 2000–2002.

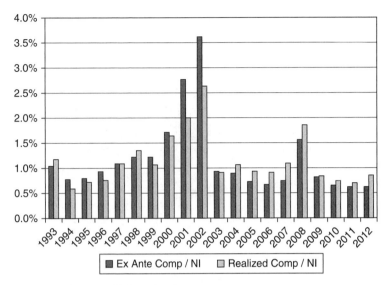

FIGURE 2.5. S&P 500 CEO pay/net income, 1993–2012
Source: ExecuComp, Compustat, calculations by Steven N. Kaplan and Joshua Rauh

How have CEOs done relative to others? There is no question that CEOs are paid a lot relative to the typical household or worker. The question that we wanted to ask is, has their pay increased in an outsized way relative to other high earners in the economy?

When examining the hypothesis that CEOs are expropriating shareholders or other stakeholders, one would want to examine whether the agents in the economy that we believe are most capable of setting their own pay had actually done better relative to others in the economy. Has their pay increased in an outsized way relative to other high earners with less ability to set their own pay? We can study this question by measuring CEO pay as a fraction of the very top IRS income brackets.

What I'm going to show you here is S&P 500 CEO estimated pay versus the adjusted gross income (AGI) of the average taxpayer in the top 0.1 percent, which now is about 140,000 taxpayers.

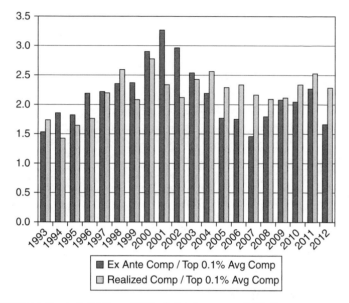

FIGURE 2.6. Ex-Ante S&P 500 CEO relative to average AGI of top 0.1 percent, 1993–2012

Source: ExecuComp, Piketty and Saez data, calculations by Steven N. Kaplan and Joshua Rauh

Figure 2.6 shows that the S&P 500 CEOs are not representing more of this top 0.1 percent of income than they have in the past. There is some up and down that is related probably to the stock market, the timing of when options are granted, and how they are valued. But this is not a graph that is consistent with the notion that CEOs are occupying a lot more of these top income echelons than in the past. If anything, it looks fairly flat.

Under the usual rents story, we would hypothesize that public CEOs would particularly profit because of agency problems related to dispersed ownership. The rents hypothesis is predicated on the ability of CEOs to control their own pay to some extent, rather than be subject to market forces. What do we see? CEO pay has increased along with the rest of the top of the income distribution, but CEOs are no more represented in the top of the income distribution than they were a couple of decades ago. CEOs in 2010 through 2012 are taking home a smaller share of corporate net income than in most previous years. The broad conclusion here is that the rise in top 1 percent incomes is not a phenomenon that is particular to CEOs of public companies whose shareholders are not disciplining them.

What about private company executives? There is a 2012 working paper by a trio of authors (Jon Bakija, Adam Cole, and Bradley T. Heim) who accessed IRS tax returns and were able to access a coded version at the bottom of the tax return where the occupation is listed of the primary earner. They looked at income of executives and managers of businesses who are more likely to be at publicly traded companies versus private. Now, the data do not provide an actual designation of whether the manager who is filing the personal tax returns works at a public or private firm. They do provide indications of whether the managers are salaried or derive their income from the profits of closely held firms. Bakija et al. are therefore imputing whether the firm is public or private on the basis of whether the filer of the tax returns is indicating that the income comes from salaries or from the business income of closely held firms.

As figure 2.7 shows, sourced from the Bakija et al. paper, the percent of total income from executives, managers, and supervisors in the top 0.1 percent has increased a lot. That percentage has gone from 0.5 percent up to around 2.5 percent. For salaried executives, who are more likely at the publicly traded companies, there is little or no trend.

So the Bakija et al. data show that private-company executives are representing a larger share of the very top income brackets than before. Again, the salaried ones, those would be the ones who would tend to be in publicly traded companies, have been flat.

What can we conclude from this? There have clearly been larger pay increases for executives of private, closely held companies

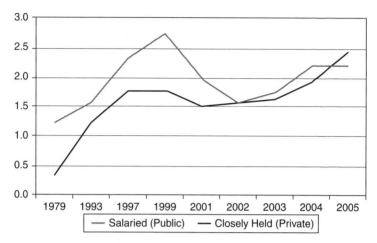

FIGURE 2.7. Percentage of total income from executives, managers, and supervisors in top 0.1 percent

Source: Jon Bakija, Adam Cole, and Bradley T. Heim, "Jobs and Income Growth of Top Earners and the Causes of Changing Income Inequality: Evidence from US Tax Return Data," April 2012, Tables 6 and 7

than for public CEOs. That is not broadly consistent with the rents hypothesis. Theory would say that there are fewer agency problems and fewer managerial power issues at the privately held companies than at the closely held businesses, because the closely held businesses are the ones where the owners are the managers. We don't have a problem of the separation between ownership and control that economic theory tells us drives these agency problems.

Of course, there could also be agency problems in privately held companies. Those would typically be between majority shareholders and minority shareholders. At the end of the day, you have to figure that there is a market that these firms face. They're producing some kind of product. The market is telling them what kinds of profits that they can earn. Unless there's been some kind of drastic increase in market power, it's hard to see how this can be consistent with a rent-seeking hypothesis. In addition, private executives

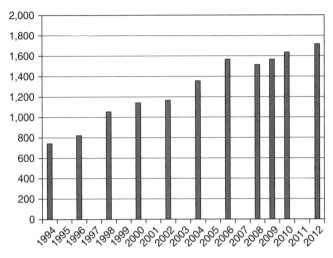

FIGURE 2.8. Average profit per partner at top 50 US law firms, 1994–2012 (in thousands of 2012 dollars)

Source: The American Lawyer magazine, calculations by Kaplan and Rauh

don't have to disclose their pay, but public executives do. So this evidence doesn't really fit the changing social norms story that well, either.

Next, we look at other occupations. If it's not the CEOs, then who is it that's occupying these top income brackets?

The next set of figures I am going to show you considers lawyers at top law firms, another useful comparison group. Since 1994, what has happened to top law partner pay? Figure 2.8 shows average profit per partner at the top fifty law firms. It was around $750,000 in 1994, and around $1.7 million in 2012. This is all in inflation-adjusted dollars. So lawyers have done particularly well. This is a strong and steady increase, in contrast to CEO pay, which has been up and down.

What about lawyers relative to the top 0.1 percent? Figure 2.9 shows that lawyer incomes are countercyclical. If you look at where the local highs in this are, it's during times where the rest of the

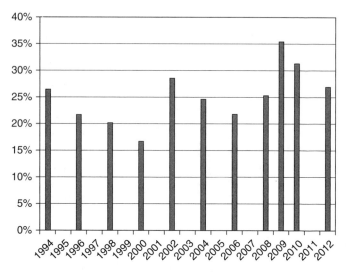

FIGURE 2.9. Average profit/partner at top 50 law firms relative to average AGI of top 0.1%, 1994–2012

Source: The American Lawyer magazine, calculations by Kaplan and Rauh

economy is not doing so well. So, lawyers tend to look really good during a time period when the economy and the stock market are not generating the kinds of returns that they may have been generating in other times. Overall, lawyers' pay has not shown any clear trend relative to the top 0.1 percent, representing around 25 percent in normal times.

So far, we've seen CEO pay as flat relative to the top 1 percent. Lawyers are also basically flat relative to the top 0.1 percent. We have seen that the managers in private companies have increased their representation in the top 0.1 percent. Let's keep going.

What about hedge-fund managers? Figure 2.10 shows the hedge-fund managers, and here we have to use a whole different scale. Here we're doing multiples of pay of the top twenty-five hedge-fund managers in the economy (tabulated by the *Alpha* magazine "rich list"), relative to the sum total ex-ante pay of all 500 S&P 500 CEOs. We're looking at a different magnitude. If you

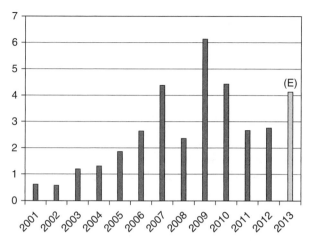

FIGURE 2.10. Multiples of pay of top twenty-five hedge-fund managers to total ex-ante pay of all 500 S&P 500 CEOs

Source: ExecuComp, *Alpha* magazine "rich lists," calculations by Kaplan and Rauh

looked at these data going back to around 2001 or 2002, you have multiples of pay of around a half. So, what that means is that, if you compare the total pay of the top twenty-five hedge-fund managers in 2001 with the total pay of all 500 S&P 500 CEOs in 2001, you would find that the top twenty-five hedge-fund managers were earning about 50 percent of what the top 500 CEOs of publicly traded companies were earning.

Hedge-fund pay went up quite dramatically in the early 2000s. It did so in a partially cyclical way, but it is perhaps more so a volatility phenomenon. By 2007, the top twenty-five hedge-fund managers were earning more than four times total S&P 500 CEO pay. They peak in 2009 at around six times. Hedge-fund managers like volatility. They didn't like 2011 or 2012 as much, where they were earning two or three times what all of the S&P 500 CEOs were earning, still a very high level of pay but smaller compared to surrounding years. In 2013, we don't have the denominator yet, but the estimate is about four times.

The top hedge-fund managers are the individuals who are likely to be at the very top of the pay scale. In fact, every year, there are a few hedge-fund managers who are earning more than $1 billion per year.

What do the hedge-fund manager results say about the theories? That depends on the interpretation of the hedge-fund manager's activities. On the one hand, one might ask whether this finance is a form of rent-seeking. It might be. I'm a finance professor, but I still admit that not all financial market activities are about making markets more efficient. On the other hand, a lot of hedge-fund activity is voluntary purchase of financial services by wealthy individuals who are the clients of hedge-fund managers. A lot of clients are university endowments. A lot of clients are rich individuals. They invest with hedge funds and pay fees because they like the distribution of outcomes that they believe hedge-fund managers are offering them. Many hedge funds offer zero-beta (market-neutral) or negative-beta portfolios. The clients of these hedge funds are willing to pay "two-and-twenty" for these investment opportunities. The investments are voluntary investments by extremely wealthy economic agents, and hedge-fund managers are receiving their fees from the resources of those extremely wealthy agents for providing services that those agents appear to value.

The only place where I would think of the hedge-fund manager as expropriating the general public is possibly in some of the poorer hedge-fund investments that have been made by public-sector pension funds. But that's something that the government is deciding, and over which the government has control.

So one possibility is that the government is making the public better off by investing public resources in hedge funds, which provide a desirable distribution of investment outcomes. The other possibility is that they're making the public worse off and are at fault for investing money with managers who are not creating value.

The bottom line is that it's hard to see how there's a direct chain of expropriation by hedge-fund managers in which hedge-fund managers expropriate the general public. The only way that could happen is via some kind of action that the government takes by having public-sector pension funds invest in poorly performing hedge funds.

Professor Kaplan and I also looked at professional athletes. I haven't updated this as recently. The data in figure 2.11 go through 2011. Top professional athletes have also seen their pay go up by a great deal. Depending on which team you're a fan of, you might perhaps view LeBron James as expropriating the general public through his basketball-playing. But the fact that his salary is so high is the result of a market for his talent, not a financial expropriation. Why is it that professional baseball, basketball, and football players earn so much more money now than they did twenty years ago? That is most likely related to what the market is willing to pay for their talent.

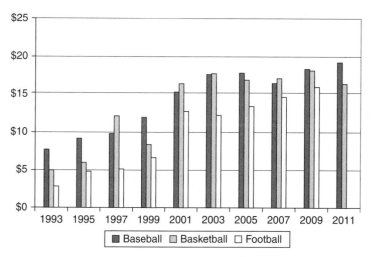

FIGURE 2.11. Average top twenty-five salaries in professional baseball, basketball, and football (in millions of 2010 dollars)

Source: Steven N. Kaplan and Joshua Rauh

So in sports, as in other occupations, there isn't really a sense in which managerial power is influencing top pay here. The overall point is that the pay increases have been really pervasive at the top. We think the evidence is consistent with scale and super-stars effects. We think that's evidence that it's consistent with skill-biased technological change where you have executives, investors, lawyers, athletes, and other talented people in the economy who can apply their talent over larger companies, larger asset pools, and larger audiences than ever before. There's clearly an element of globalization that contributes as well, as that contributes to making the markets that talented individuals can reach much larger. Overall, we find the evidence on the occupations consistent with "It's-the-Market" and not with the "Rents-of-the-Powerful" hypothesis.

The other set of analyses on which we've been working to shed light on the various income inequality theories looks at wealth-generating activities of the Forbes lists. So, we examine the top 400 wealthiest individuals in the US. We have done this over four samples: 1982, 1992, 2001, and 2011. These were the years for which we have the data. We're working on filling in the intermittent years. We also have Forbes lists of global billionaires from 1987, 1992, 2001, and 2012.

There are four main questions that we address. First, of the top 400 wealthiest individuals in the United States, did they own first-generation businesses or inherited businesses? Second, did the individuals grow up wealthy or not? Third, were they well-educated? And fourth, what industries were they in?

What we're trying to get is the question of how much wealth of the super-wealthy is inherited or generated by the capital of their parents, and how much is generated by their own work, ingenuity, or innovation. Figure 2.12 examines the generation of wealth-creating businesses in the Forbes 400. On the bottom axis are the generation numbers. So, for example, Facebook, a first-

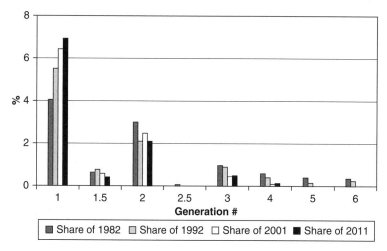

FIGURE 2.12. Generation of wealth-creating business in Forbes 400: more self-made, less inheritance

Source: Steven N. Kaplan and Joshua Rauh

generation business, would be given a one. A two is a business that was founded by the member of the Forbes 400's mother or father. A three would be a business that was founded by a member of the Forbes 400's grandmother or grandfather. What is one and a half? A half is where you could argue that the parent founded the business, but the member of the Forbes 400 grew the business dramatically.

The different shaded bars show, over the different samples of the different time periods, what the generation was. So, in the Forbes 400 in 1982, first-generation businesses made up 40 percent of the list. By the 2011 Forbes 400, it was around 65 percent to 70 percent. That means that more businesses in the Forbes 400 were self-made, first-generation businesses. What are the categories where it decreased? Second generation, third generation, and fourth generation all decreased. There are no fifth and sixth generations in the later Forbes 400 years, whereas in the 1982 lists, some of the super-wealthy were still deriving their wealth from businesses that had

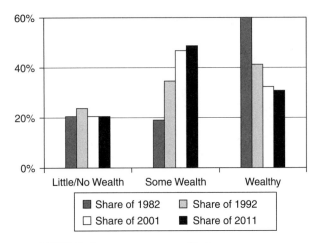

FIGURE 2.13. Did US Forbes 400 grow up wealthy?

Source: Steven N. Kaplan and Joshua Rauh

been started by Rockefellers and Vanderbilts. Those Rockefellers and Vanderbilts were still in the Forbes 400 in 1982, but they're not there today. We interpret that as meaning that inheritance is becoming less important in determining top wealth levels.

What about whether they grew up wealthy? Figure 2.13 shows the US Forbes 400 and whether they grew up wealthy. The categories we collected were: little or no wealth, some wealth, or wealthy. So Bill Gates grew up with some wealth. His father was a lawyer, not a rich businessman. That gives you the idea of what we're trying to do here. Obviously, the Rockefellers, they grew up wealthy. So, we collected information about their family history and assessed whether they grew up wealthy.

What we find is that the Forbes 400 is basically flat in terms of the percentage over time who grew up with little or no wealth. Some wealth is the category that went up from 20 percent to around 45 percent to 50 percent. Growing up wealthy became much less important. So, it is true that the Forbes 400 grew up in what I would describe as upper-middle-class backgrounds. The children

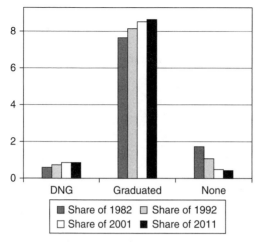

FIGURE 2.14. Higher education of Forbes 400

Source: Steven N. Kaplan and Joshua Rauh

of upper-middle-class people make up a much greater portion of the Forbes 400 in the later years than they did in the early '80s.

And then, what about education? Well, that's kind of a no-brainer. Education is more important. Figure 2.14 shows three categories: went to college but did not graduate, graduated from college, or had no education. No education, which was always a small portion, has gone down. Graduated from college was always a large portion, but it's gone up. Education has become even more important. So, that's not going to be surprising to many in this room.

We also looked at the industries. From what industries are the Forbes 400 making their money? Not surprisingly, technology—and especially computer technology—was a very big category. Another category that has seen strong growth and represents a full 15 percent of the 2011 Forbes 400 is retail and restaurants. We also view this as being consistent with scaling. Consider the founders of companies like Wal-Mart. A lot of what they're able to do is the result of being able to scale up operations in a massive way.

TABLE 2.1. Industries of US Forbes 400

	1982	1992	2001	2011	A(11-82)
Industrial					
Retail/Restaurant	0.053	0.118	0.132	0.150	+0.097
Technology—Computer	0.033	0.053	0.130	0.123	+0.090
Technology—Medical	0.005	0.018	0.021	0.023	+0.017
Consumer	0.131	0.174	0.125	0.108	−0.023
Media	0.136	0.132	0.164	0.100	−0.036
Diversified/Other	0.207	0.205	0.156	0.123	−0.084
Energy	0.214	0.089	0.062	0.098	−0.117
Finance and Investments					
Hedge Funds	0.005	0.011	0.018	0.075	+0.070
Private Equity/LBO	0.018	0.034	0.039	0.068	+0.050
Money Management	0.018	0.055	0.062	0.045	+0.027
Venture Capital	0.003	0.005	0.008	0.015	+0.012
Real Estate	0.179	0.105	0.081	0.075	−0.104

Source: Steven N. Kaplan and Joshua Rauh

What industries have declined in their representation among the Forbes 400? Energy has actually gone down. So, companies that are endowed with natural resources and selling energy do not represent nearly as much of the Forbes 400 as they did before. In 1982, energy was 21 percent; 2011 is around 10 percent. Some of that drop is the result of the grandchildren of the energy titans dropping out of the Forbes 400 sample in more recent years.

Finance is also very important. Hedge-fund managers were basically zero in 1982. In 2011, they're now 7.5 percent of the Forbes 400. That came at the expense of real estate, which has gone down.

The conclusion is that extensive family wealth and inheritance have become less important, while access to education has become more important. There are very few people in the top 400 now without any college education. What about industry evidence? The premium for technological skill is continuing to rise at the very top. Retail, technology, and finance are increasing. Real estate and energy are decreasing. We interpret that as being consistent with the idea that skilled individuals are applying talent to larger blocks of capital. That's also related to finance. Finance is up from 4.5 percent in 1982 to 20 percent in 2011 of the Forbes 400. Also, in terms of the timing—except for finance—a lot of these changes occurred by 2001.

Finally, we also looked outside of the United States and examined the Forbes global billionaire lists. We found that the share of global billionaires who are first-generation also rose by a similar amount abroad as in the US. The technology component became more important globally, but its rise was not as strong as in the US. In stark contrast to the US, the category that gained the most globally in producing the billionaires is mining, metals, and energy. We believe that what's going on there is something about the initial allocation of property rights in developing countries. So that is one divergence between the global story and the US story, although the technology component is very important globally. (As an aside, I would note that many of the people in the Forbes 400 US list actually weren't born in the US.)

Figure 2.15 shows that the non-US billionaires were much more likely to grow up with little or no wealth than the US billionaires.

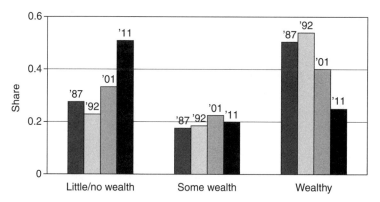

FIGURE 2.15. Outside the US: Sharpest difference between wealthiest individuals in United States and around the world?

Source: Who's Who and Internet searches

Remember that for the US super-wealthy, the category that grew was "some wealth." Both in the US and across the world, the rich are less likely than before to have grown up wealthy. In terms of the global billionaires, they are actually more likely to have grown up with little or no wealth, both in comparison to the US and in comparison to the way global wealth was generated thirty years ago.

So to conclude, those are the facts that I wanted to present. We're interpreting the facts and asking with which model are they the most consistent. Our interpretation is that the main drivers of increased income inequality in the US are technological change, increased scale, and their interaction. In sum: "It's the Market." That also has a very important educational component. Globalization may have contributed as well. Most changes occurred before 2000, and there hasn't been a recent acceleration of trends in a lot of these categories. Also, in the developing world, clearly there's something going on with the reallocation of property rights. Although again, there are a lot more people in the world at large who are billionaires now who grew up with little or no wealth.

Question and Answer

QUESTION: *It seems like your research showed that the returns to skill have exploded since the 1980s. I know that you haven't looked at the time period previous to that, but what's your explanation for why that changed in the 1980s—if indeed it did change—where the returns have gone up so drastically compared to the previous decades?*

RAUH: I think that it's a mix of things. We're not able to disentangle all of them. Two major factors come to mind. First of all, skill-biased technological change and the fact that the demand for skilled labor relative to the supply of skilled labor has taken off since the 1980s. Second is the massive scale of the impact that computers and information technology have had since the 1980s, which allows talent to multiply across a much larger scale.

QUESTION: *It looks like the only smoking gun in your evidence is the hedge-fund guys. If you sort of look through the data, everything else is clean. Everybody else is the market, but the two-and-twenty always struck me as hard to understand as an equilibrium configuration, especially given the data that you and your other finance colleagues present to us on how ineffective money managers are at actually raising rates of return. So, I'm wondering whether you see this as either sort of a temporary phenomenon, a temporary anomaly, or whether there's something having to do with selection in the way that you're just looking at the top guys, and that just tends to be a more skewed distribution, and maybe we should be looking at something else.*

RAUH: Well, that is a very interesting question. To answer it, we have to look at who are the main investors in hedge funds. It's public-sector pension funds, university endowments, and wealthy individuals. Essentially, hedge funds are earning two-and-twenty off of these investors who have been willing to invest their money with hedge funds despite these apparently generous compensation contracts.

Now, I am sure that you've seen the news that the California Public Employees' Retirement System (CalPERS) is pulling out of hedge funds entirely, with plans to divest $4 billion of hedge-fund positions. And one of the reasons that hedge funds have come under fire lately, at CalPERS and elsewhere, is that if you had followed the John Bogle approach over the past five years and just invested in the stock market, you'd have made phenomenal returns since the financial crisis.

Recent history is leading to a backlash. Some hedge funds are investing in strategies that are not correlated with the market and that will do very well in tail events, but not when the market is climbing. Some of them did very well in 2009. Other hedge funds are probably just investing in assets that basically have betas equal to one or more, and are collecting two-and-twenty for making those investments.

I think that there's probably going to be some refinement of the industry. CalPERS has apparently decided that it's not worth it for them. Perhaps they have come under political pressure, and people say, "Look how well the public markets have done. Why didn't you do this well in hedge funds?" Some observers have not been doing any kind of beta correction or asking in what kinds of market environments hedge funds are supposed to be doing well.

So, yes, the willingness of wealthy individuals and of wealthy institutions to pay two-and-twenty is something of a puzzle, and is a big piece of the top if you look at the top 0.1 percent. Hedge-fund people are highly represented there.

QUESTION: *On one of your early slides, you put a comparison. As I recall, it had calendar years on the horizontal axis of your ex-ante estimate of pay, basically including the Black-Scholes value of options, or the current value of restricted stock, even though it's restricted and realized. As I recall, it showed that the ex-ante estimates were usually quite a bit higher than the ex-post estimates. Now, as I understand it, they're not really referring to the same granting of grants. Have you ever tried to look at going back a few years [at] what actually happened and at how you would compare the ex-ante with the ex-post? What goes on in the market and [with] the individual stock, the implied volatility and the formula? I think that that would be interesting as well.*

RAUH: You're exactly right. In terms of the timing, the ex-ante is measured using Black-Scholes. It's the market value as the date the options were granted. The ex-post is the realized value when they were exercised. And so that does affect the time patterns. We could try to decompose these differences into how much of the difference is due to timing and how much is due to valuation.

QUESTION: *In terms of technological change, I guess that you usually tend to think of technology like the production function, but I was wondering if you could comment on the extent to which you think that some of the key technological changes about which you're thinking are like the market technology, whether it's improvements in the capital market or improvement in the market for control or franchising. All of these things seem to be really tightly related, not just to traditional production-function type of technologies, but to market technologies. In some sense, improvement of the market may play a role in some of the things that you're seeing and looking at here.*

RAUH: As a finance guy, I think a lot about financial market technologies, which in some ways have gotten more efficient and allow managers to manage much larger pools of capital than they could have in the past. Of course, there have been more controversial innovations in market technology like high-frequency trading. That has earned a lot of money for some people, though it's not clear what the value of that actually is. I think that it's a very useful distinction, and even though we've been working on this for a while, I still feel like we're at that very beginning of understanding why it is that we see these changes as being so broad-based and what kinds of changes in technology are actually driving it.

QUESTION: *Have you looked at the relationship between top pay in a corporation and the pay of people who are close, but not at the top? That is, the top pay is public. It does create some restriction, I think. But sometimes, and I've observed in some cases, you have to get the top guy to get his pay up in order to allow people below him to get their pay up. So, there's a push. Have you explored that or run into that?*

RAUH: We worked on this a little bit. We tried to do some exercises where we know the total compensation for firms. We know what the top managers earn. We tried to do some modeling of what we think. What are various possibilities for the distribution of pay of the managers below the top five in a publicly traded company? We parameterized it in different ways. Ultimately we couldn't really find a big impact of managers below the top five in the company on these types of very top quintile statistics, even looking at a range of possible intra-firm distributions of pay. The study that I mentioned that uses IRS data also makes progress on that as well because they measure whether an executive is salaried or whether they're part of a closely held corporation. There you see the salaried share of the top 0.1 percent going down. That includes all salaried, and not just salaried whose pay is observable in ExecuComp among the top five executives. And so, that also suggests that, when it comes to the corporate managers, they're not really the driving force behind the story.

QUESTION: On hedge funds, the first comment to make is that two-and-twenty is the rack rate in a hedge fund. There's a limited amount of publication and especially of hedge-fund contracts with public pensions like the state of New Jersey. You'll find that they get a rather better deal, so you have to be a little bit careful about that. But the research on returns to hedge funds, to my knowledge, doesn't reject the possibility that these guys are actually earning what they're taking from it in the sense that, if you look at what hedge funds deliver to their limited partners, the returns are within striking distance at least of the risk-adjusted benchmark. Now, on this question of the disclosure of publicly traded executives, AIG had this very clever idea. They created a privately held, independent corporation that hired all of the executives, and then they wrote a service contract with AIG. So far as I know, no other publicly traded company has copied that. The fact that they haven't copied it, and that AIG got away with it, suggests that maybe there isn't rent-seeking. It supports your theory, I think, that it's the market.

RAUH: I guess that I would just add to your comment about hedge funds that if indeed what hedge funds are providing are very good returns during very bad and very volatile states of the world, then they are providing a valuable service that investors want. Investors are willing to invest in them because it expands the investable space for them. In reality, of course, there's a wide range of strategies that the hedge funds are pursuing. So, some of them are doing that, and some of them may be doing other things.

QUESTION: *One of the nice things about being able to test these two different theories is in principle it helps you to figure out what kind of policy is appropriate. But within the "It's the Market," there's a bunch of different things going on: globalization, skill-biased tech-nological change, etc. It seems to me that we need to know a little bit more about which of those are driving this in order to think about the policy implications, but maybe not. Maybe there are some already about which you can speculate.*

RAUH: Well, I agree. There are going to be some areas where information technology is very clearly playing a role in skill-biased technological change, and others where globalization and access to large pools of capital are more important. I think that we could probably do some decomposition of that based on what we've done before, but more research is going to be needed for that.

QUESTION: *I just wanted to go back to hedge funds for a second. One important point is that it's never the same hedge-fund* manager in the top year after year. The "twenty part" means the guy who got lucky. We all know that the persistence there is very small. Whereas with the CEO, you get to be in that top for four or five years in a row. I think that that may be pushing a lot of it. On the fees, I asked a hedge-fund manager who is a friend of mine to defend his crazy fees. His answer was that we give you something like momentum, which you don't know how to trade, and the two-and-twenty of highly leveraged portfolio is like 2 percent off of the top of a long-only portfolio. That was his defense of the fees. I'm not sure if it's a good defense, but as you point out, it's all of our endowments investing in them.

RAUH: There is actually a good deal of persistence within the list of the highest-earning hedge-fund managers. It's not as much as in the CEOs, that's true, but there is a good deal of persistence, due to the growth in the amount of capital the most successful hedge-fund managers have under management. You certainly have the John Paulsons of the world who made one great bet in 2009, and then a worse one in 2010, and so if it were just about one-year performance he'd be off the list in 2010. But it is not just about one-year performance, because of the management fee.

QUESTION: I don't know how closely you looked at the international data, but the interesting thing to me was how few people were in the wealthy category to start. Between 1982 and the present, there's been gigantic change in China. I don't know if you've looked very closely at the geographic thing. Also, one could argue, and this may be anecdotal, that gigantic change has occurred in Russia, too, with oligarchs. Have you had a chance to look at countries and at what's going on there?

RAUH: Yes, we can do some decomposition. However, for these global billionaires the data set is not that big. This cutoff at a billion is a bit of a challenge for us. Many of the factors you mention could be operating simultaneously. Note that some of the oligarchs did not exactly grow up wealthy either. They may have grown up powerful or as parts of powerful families, but they had opportunities to grab property rights when they were available. In China, in contrast, there are some who are very much self-made capitalists. Those are very distinct stories.

CHAPTER THREE

The Economic Determinants of Top Income Inequality

Charles I. Jones

What I've been spending my time on for the last couple years is something that I think was very much in the Gary Becker tradition of economics, which is if you want to understand something, then an important part of that understanding is being able to write down models of rational economic agents, where the phenomenon that you're studying emerges in the model. You ought to be able to build an economy in which the phenomenon happens. So I've been thinking about the kind of assumptions we need to make in order to build economies where top income inequality rises dramatically in the United States after being flat for thirty years before, but stays pretty flat in France.

Figure 3.1 shows a picture that we're all familiar with when talking about income inequality: the income share of the top 0.1 percent starting from a common value in the US and France from 1950 to 1980 of around 2.5 percent or 3 percent, rising quite dramatically in the US up to 8 or 9 percent. And in contrast, the top income share stays quite low in France.

Figure 3.2 shows you the top 1 percent share in the early eighties on the horizontal axis, and the top 1 percent share in the mid-2000s on the vertical axis, together with a 45-degree line. And this chart uses the data that Emmanuel Saez and Thomas Piketty put together. What you can see in this graph—which I think is quite remarkable—is that the rise in income inequality is not just a US phenomenon. It's happening everywhere in the world for which we

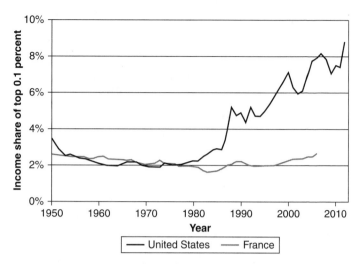

FIGURE 3.1. Top income inequality in the United States and France

Source: Charles I. Jones and Jihee Kim, "A Schumpeterian Model of Top Income Inequality," *NBER Paper No. 20637,* October 2014, figure 1

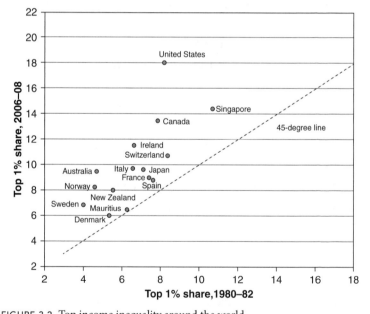

FIGURE 3.2. Top income inequality around the world

Source: Charles I. Jones and Jihee Kim, "A Schumpeterian Model of Top Income Inequality," *NBER Paper No. 20637,* October 2014, figure 3

have data over these two periods. Yet there's heterogeneity in the extent of the rise. You see an increase in top income and inequality even in Sweden, even in France, and it's just the magnitude of the inequality differences that stand out. But inequality is rising everywhere, which suggests to me there is something broad-based going on, and that appealing to narrow features of the US economy, for example, is likely to give you an incomplete explanation of the phenomenon.

Since Pareto created his distribution more than a century ago, it's been appreciated that the top of the income distribution looks like a Pareto distribution. If you want to think about a model of top income inequality, you're inevitably drawn to consider Pareto distributions. What figure 3.3 shows is that top incomes in the US are consistent with the Pareto distribution. Suppose we pick a cutoff, let's say $500,000 a year. Now consider all the taxpayers who make more than $500,000 a year, and figure out what the average of their incomes is. Look at that as a ratio to the $500,000

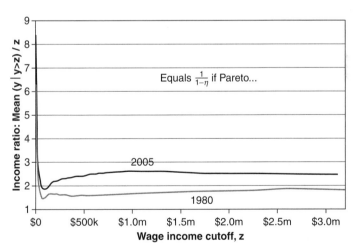

FIGURE 3.3. The Pareto nature of labor income

Source: Charles I. Jones and Jihee Kim, "A Schumpeterian Model of Top Income Inequality," *NBER Paper No. 20637,* October 2014, figure 5

cutoff. It turns out that number is about two and a half in 2005. Now move the cutoff. Look at everyone above a million, everyone above a million and a half, look at the average of the incomes above the cutoff, and divide it by the cutoff. For a Pareto distribution, it's a constant, and that's what you see in this graph. Moreover, in 1980, that same statistic is flat at a value of sort of one and a half or one and three quarters, once you get above, say, $250,000 or $300,000. In 2005, instead, the ratio is flat at a number more like two and a half.

The notion that top incomes are Pareto jumps out at you from the data. That's true for labor income. Let me spend just a minute on connecting Pareto distributions with the kind of numbers that Piketty and Saez and others have made famous now, which are the share of income going to the top 1 percent.

It turns out, there's a one-to-one mapping between a key parameter of the Pareto distribution and those top 1 percent shares. A Pareto distribution says, what fraction of people have incomes above Y? Well, that's just Y raised to some power. And if you let $S(P)$ be the share of income going to the top P percent, so $S(1)$ is the top 1 percent share, it turns out that's just $100/P$ raised to some power. And the key power there is this parameter called η, it's a key parameter of the Pareto distribution, and basically if η is a half, then the share of income going to the top 1 percent is 10 percent. If η is three quarters, the share of income going to the top 1 percent is a third. And you can move that thing around and can get different shares. The point is that, if you want to write down a model where we can make sense of the data, what you're going to need is to write down a model where the data generate a Pareto distribution for incomes, and where the exponent in that Pareto distribution is changing. That's what you need to get out of a model. That's the kind of thing I'm thinking about.

One of the neat things about the Pareto distribution, and one of the neat things about the income data, is that it has a fractal pattern. So if you ask, "What share of the top 10 percent's income goes to the top 1 percent?" that's some number. Which share of the top 1 percent's income goes to the top tenth? That's some number. What share of the top tenth goes to the top hundredth? That's some number. It turns out, with a Pareto distribution, they are all the same number. And as top income and inequality rise, that same number is rising over time.

To get these Pareto distributions, to get a theory about why that Pareto exponent is changing, is relatively straightforward. And people have been thinking about this in many contexts for a number of years. The key insight is that exponential growth and Pareto distributions tend to go hand-in-hand. When you have one, you often get the other.

Imagine we have some entrepreneurs. Suppose you're out there, sitting in your mom's basement eating ramen noodles, trying to write an iPhone app. You finally write the new iPhone app, it gets posted on the iTunes store, and you get some income, some people start buying it. But initially, there aren't that many people buying it. Your initial income is low. And then, as you've worked hard, as you've continued marketing your app, your income rises, and it rises exponentially at some growth rate. That's the exponential growth.

The second piece of the intuition is that you need exponential growth to occur for an exponentially distributed amount of time. That's a fancy way of saying something that's really simple, which is, say there's some probability that your business dies every period. By death in this entrepreneurial sense, we just mean somebody else comes along, and they were writing an iPhone app in their basement, and now they kick you off the top hundred list of the iTunes app store, and they're the next Angry Birds, and you're the old Angry Birds. There's some constant probability that this happens every period. It turns out, if you put these two things together, you get a Pareto distribution. And the key Pareto exponent turns out to be the ratio of the growth rate to the death rate.

The way this works in a graph is fairly straightforward. Let x_0 denote your initial sales of the iPhone app. You're working hard. You're causing your sales to grow and it bounces around because it's kind of a random process, you have good days and bad days, good weeks and bad weeks. The more effort you put in, the faster is the growth. The faster the growth, the wider the distribution. There is going to be a bigger gap between the top person and the newest entrepreneur. So the faster the rate of exponential growth, the wider this inequality could be. And then the death rate pushes you down and kicks you out, and lets someone else start over. The higher is the death rate, well, that's going to restrain the extent to which the graph line can get away from the bottom. Exponential growth and creative destruction, which is what death corresponds to are the two forces that are operating: exponential growth pushes inequality up, while creative destruction pushes inequality down.

What we need in a richer model is a theory of what determines that growth rate, what economic forces affect the rate at which an entrepreneur's income grows, and what economic forces affect the death rate, or creative destruction. It's other people trying to come

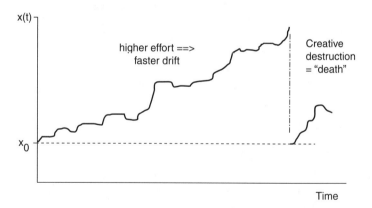

FIGURE 3.4. Basic mechanism: random growth with death → Pareto

Source: Charles I. Jones and Jihee Kim, "A Schumpeterian Model of Top Income Inequality," *NBER Paper No. 20637,* October 2014, figure 9

up with new ideas and kick you out of the market and take over your position.

These same kinds of forces apply to wealth inequality. Piketty's book has a lot of discussion about how wealth inequality depends on $r - g$, and we saw some graphs like that earlier today. It turns out—and Piketty's book is based on a model like this at some level—$r - g$ is the growth part of the wealth. If you ask, how fast is wealth growing? Well, the interest rate is the key part of that wealth, and if you're looking at wealth normalized by income to get a stationary distribution, then you're going to get wealth growing at $r - g$, and then you might incorporate taxes, and you might take into account that wealth doesn't just grow. People eat some of it, too. And so, in some sense, the growth rate is $r - g$ minus taxes, minus some consumption. And then the effective death rate has to do with births and deaths. Those deaths can be creative-destruction kind of deaths, or they could be literal deaths. Piketty makes a point that the population growth rate is an important part of the wealth distribution. This same logic gives you the kind of model that he's talking about.

I think I've given you the basic spirit of the model. We've got researchers out there, spending time in their mom's basement, eating ramen noodles, trying to write iPhone apps. When they are successful, they become entrepreneurs, and then they're building their market share. The rate at which they build their market share is going to be a top determinant of income inequality. And then the rate at which other people are out there, trying to kick them off their pedestal, that's going to be another determinant.

I don't want you to think of this model as being just about iPhone apps. When I say entrepreneurs and researchers, I mean it to apply more broadly, and you can think of different applications of how this might work. Surgeons are trying to create new surgical techniques. You're known as being the best surgeon for this kind of heart replacement surgery, and then you can sell your idea to the rest of the world. You build your market share by being success-ful and by advertising, and then someone else comes along trying to come up with a better surgical technique. Lawyers are similar, as are rock stars and musicians. Alan Krueger wrote a nice paper about the data for rock stars and top income inequality. But even middle managers are trying to come up with new business innova-tions that allow them to expand their segment of the business and get the attention of the higher-ups.

This story applies more broadly. And in some sense, connecting with what Josh Rauh was saying, one of the many useful insights of his research is that it's not just finance, it's not just CEOs, it's not just managers, it's not just athletes. It's all these people together. For top income inequality, you're not going to get one story in which it's only the hedge-fund managers. Part of it is the hedge-fund managers. But there are a lot of other people in the top who are seeing their incomes grow, and who are part of the top tenth of a percent or the top 1 percent. So you need a story that's broader. And that's what I'm trying to get at with this line of argument.

What are the economic determinants of top income inequality according to a model like this? Well, it turns out there are several of them. In a sense, one of the problems is there are too many. It's hard to get data on them, and it's hard to quantify and say, "This is really a thing that's driving change." Instead, the model highlights the kind of forces that could be driving top income inequality.

The first one to highlight is technology. I mentioned earlier that one of the key forces that increases top income inequal-ity is anything that raises the growth rate of the entrepreneurs. Think about the World Wide Web. In the old days, when you had a great idea, you sold it to the people around you. Maybe that was the end or maybe you went around and sold it to a broader audience, but it was remarkably hard to start selling to a larger and larger market. With the advent of the World Wide Web, it's become increasingly easy to grow your market very rapidly. And so your ability to grow rapidly, the returns to your effort if you're trying to grow the market rapidly, have increased enormously, and that's a worldwide force. When I look at that early graph, and I see top income inequality rising all over the world, it makes me think of technological change, and in my model, this is the kind of technological change that could lead to a rise in top income inequality.

Some of the other things are less obvious and maybe more interesting because they're less obvious. The second one is subsidies to research. Think about what a subsidy to research does in a model like this. Well, if you pay people to sit in their mom's basement writing iPhone apps, you subsidize more research. You get more people looking for new ideas, that's going to lead to more of this creative destruction. They're going to kick more people out. The death rate is going to go up. That is going to prevent the gap between the top people and the new entrepreneurs from expanding as far. That's actually going to reduce top income inequality in this setting. Research subsidies, anything that increases creative destruction, is actually going to limit top income inequality.

Conversely, you can think about blocking innovation. One of the things in the political economy of this that firms might try to do, is they may say, "We want to protect our market. We don't want to let people kick us out." And so you lobby, you set up mechanisms to protect your market. Anything that does that is going to limit creative destruction. That's going to increase top income inequality. And that would be a bad thing. So you can see there are good things and bad things. I see technology as a good thing, subsidies to research probably at the margin a good thing; blocking innovation will be a bad thing. So when you see top income inequality going up, it could be a good thing, it could be a bad thing. It depends on the forces that are behind it. That's one of the lessons that I've learned from this model.

Another example is misallocation. Imagine that in some country when entrepreneurs develop new ideas, the officials are more likely not to protect the intellectual property rights, or to take that property right and give it to a crony friend. In that case, there's more destruction. The returns to you from coming up with a new idea are lower. The returns to you from growing your market share once you have a new idea are lower, because it's going to be stolen, and then that's going to increase destruction. That is going to reduce top income inequality. Finally, consider taxes on entrepreneurial effort. Once you become one of the entrepreneurs here, a key determinant of top income inequality is the rate at which you're growing your profits. That depends on your effort. You have to work hard to do that, and anything that distorts your effort is going to affect the growth rate, and therefore affect top income inequality. And here it goes the way you naturally think. Higher taxes mean entrepreneurs put forth less effort and that lowers income inequality.

The other interesting thing that wasn't obvious in this model is that growth and inequality tend to move in opposite directions. At a casual level, it's tempting to look at the data and say, if inequality were driven by technological changes, for example, you'd expect that to increase growth and increase inequality together. When you look at the data, you don't see a correlation between growth and inequality that way.

It turns out that in my model, there are some forces that tend to make growth and inequality move in opposite directions. It's not clear they have to go in the same direction. There are two reasons. The first is one I've highlighted already, that faster growth means more creative destruction. But that means there's less time for inequality to grow—due to the higher death rate—and so you lower inequality. Entrepreneurs may work less hard to grow their market. The second force is actually less intuitive, which is that with greater inequality, research is riskier. Think about technological change like the World Wide Web. Sure, that raises the returns to being an entrepreneur, because you can now build your market share more easily. You would think that tends to make research more attractive, because if you happen to be successful as a researcher, that's going to allow you to be this great entrepreneur. That force is there.

It's also the case that if you decide to be a worker, working for one of those great entrepreneurs, you benefit from that technological change as well. Technological change raises the wages of entrepreneurs, but it also raises the wages of the people who are working for the entrepreneurs. So that doesn't shift people one direction or the other. That doesn't say you do more research or less research. What turns out to shift research here is the risk effect. If there's more inequality among entrepreneurs, the research process is riskier. You don't know if you're going to be the wildly successful one or just the normal one. So research is riskier. And risk-averse researchers tend to do less research, and that could actually decrease growth and decrease creative destruction. Greater inequality from, say, the World Wide Web could decrease growth. The linkages between growth and inequality are much more subtle than I appreciated before.

Let me conclude by giving you plausible explanations in these models for inequality in France and in the United States, the graph that I began with. In rising US inequality and, to some extent, rising worldwide inequality, there's lots of evidence that technologies are a part of the story. The ability to sell to larger markets, the ability to grow your market share because of information technology, has got to be part of the story. That comes through very clearly in a model like this. That's a worldwide phenomenon, not just something about the United States, and so we'd expect it to raise inequality everywhere.

Second thing: lower taxes on top income. We've seen a decline in the top marginal tax rate in the US. It's possible that that increases effort by entrepreneurs and increases inequality, having ambiguous effects on growth in this framework. One has to be a little careful with this statement, however. The way taxes affect effort in our models is not nearly as clear as I think it is in the data. The data, I think, are pretty clear that there's an effect there. However, because substitution and income effects tend to cancel, it's a little harder to get taxes to affect top inequality in a model like this.

Then, what about France? I played with a lot of different models as I've been working this project for the last three years. And a lot of times I would get situations where rising inequality in the US is good because of technological change, and the fact that France hasn't let their inequality rise is bad, because they're resisting that technological change. It turns out in this framework that I have now, it's more subtle than that. That could be what's going on. It could be that France is delaying the adoption of good technologies, and that would clearly be a bad thing. Or it could be there's increased misallocation. Maybe they're killing off entrepreneurs more quickly, and that's causing inequality not to rise with technology.

On the other hand, there could be efficiency-enhancing explanations. Maybe it's the case that France is subsidizing research. We tend to do too little research in lots of settings. If France subsidizes research, that's going to result in more creative destruction. A higher death rate is going to kill people off, and that's going to lower inequality. So that could be going on in France. Or, it could be that France has reduced the blocking of innovations. Maybe in France these older firms were really protected. They didn't let competitors come in. Maybe France has relaxed this protection so that there's less blocking of innovations. That means there's more creative destruction and, again, that would tend to restrain inequality. Looking at the data through the lens of this model, the bottom line is it's not clear what's going on. We have stories where France could be doing the right thing or France could be doing a bad thing, and similar for the US as well.

To conclude: what are the policy implications? From my standpoint, the policy implications are relatively unclear in that I don't know which of these things is driving the rise in inequality. On the other hand, the one thing I'll say—that again was something that emerged fairly clearly from the kind of models I was playing with—is that policies that encourage research in this framework tend to lead to more growth and more creative destruction. Creative destruction tends to restrain inequality. And in general in these kinds of models, policies that encourage research are a good idea. And so even if inequality is not something we care about directly, I think it's the case that if you adopt policies that encourage research, one byproduct will be restraining the rise in inequality.

Question and Answer Session

QUESTION: *I was thinking a little bit about the interpretation of death and I was wondering whether one of the ways that there can be death in the model is people moving outside of the country. And one example is that anecdotally wealthy people have been moving out of France, perhaps to London, perhaps to the United States, because of maybe either perceptions about the tax code or perceptions about the business climate. So, for example, the population of the United Kingdom has increased over the last ten years by about 9 percent. The percentage increase of French people living in the UK has been about 50 percent. I was wondering if one can potentially use your model to explain different countries' changes in income inequality by also considering what drives people to stay and go. It may be about perceptions about tax policy. It may be about perceptions of the business climate.*

JONES: My coauthor on this research project did some work on taxes and top income inequality. I was struck by how low the top marginal tax rates were in France and how much they'd fallen. When she looked at feeding in tax rates into the model, you get a lot less action out than I would have expected. My casual impression is tax rates were high in the 1970s everywhere, and they came down a lot in the US, and maybe not so much in France, and that's right in line with the movements in inequality. You can get something along those lines. But it was not nearly as much as my casual impression led me to believe. But certainly part of the explanation for why top inequality hasn't risen so much in some of those economies could easily be related to the fact that people are leaving to avoid higher taxes and particularly the threat of higher taxes or the perception they may be higher in the future.

QUESTION: *Chad, your model does focus on those creative destruction roles so importantly. And maybe one of the things that could be going on here in thinking about it as you presented it, is technology preventing creative destruction against your own product. It could be changing the product or improving. And you can see that in some social media. I wonder if that might be something you can comment on or test for it at some point?*

JONES: Yes, I think that's a great point. Anything that blocks creative destruction, and to me I think businesses have lots of incentives to try to block that, would work along those lines. One of the facts that is related is shown in a graph that I didn't have time to put up. It was something that Steve Davis and John Haltiwanger have worked on: business dynamism in the US. And the fact that I find completely striking but which is consistent with this kind of connection is job creation and job destruction. You see a downward trend in that since 1980 in the US. If you ask, what fraction of employment is due to young firms, there's a downward trend, and it's true across industries.

It's remarkably robust. And that would be another thing that could lead to a rise in inequality in this kind of setting.

QUESTION: *Given the horizon a model like yours would likely have, why would you make such a stark distinction between level and growth effects? Because a lot of level effects are going to look like growth effects when you actually go to the data with this. The other thing I wanted to think about in that regard is linking this up to what we had in the previous paper, which is a lot more first-generation people, all these other things, which in some sense would say destruction is on the rise. And I would also go back to what I said before, which is all the market changes and other things, and how those would feed into your model. The guy who's in the basement can get funded a lot faster than he could compared with 1950. When Ray Kroc took on McDonald's, it took a long time to develop. In today's world, Five Guys can expand a lot faster because of all the improvements in capital markets. How would that fit into your model?*

CHAD JONES: I think that's right. On the level effect and the growth effects, that's exactly right. It turns out in this model, solving for the transition dynamics is not easy. It's a model of heterogeneous agents, so it's got the usual kind of problems, so that's why I haven't done it.

On the McDonald's and the Five Guys and the dynamism point, I'm with you. Casual introspection, certainly living in Silicon Valley, you have to think: what's a more dynamic place? Things are more dynamic than they have ever been.

CHAPTER FOUR

Intergenerational Mobility and Income Inequality

Jörg L. Spenkuch

My remarks today are based on recent work with the late Gary Becker, Kevin Murphy, and Scott Kominers (see Becker et al. 2014). It bears emphasizing that Gary has already written the two seminal papers in the literature on intergenerational mobility and income equality (Becker and Tomes 1979, 1986). Yet, he felt it was worth going back and giving these issues more thought. Although the economics of our analysis are very simple—in fact, we rely only on basic price theory—the conclusions that we derive differ radically from those in the literature.

Before delving into the analysis, let us start out with some simple facts that others have documented (see Corak 2013a, Corak and Heisz 1999, Mazumder 2005, among others). These facts cover much of what is currently known about intergenerational mobility in the United States and elsewhere. After presenting the facts, I will lay out a simple theory in order to make sense of the data and to link intergenerational persistence of economic status with cross-sectional inequality. Lastly, I will discuss the role of government spending in reducing both. In particular, I will be asking how governments can achieve these goals, given the economics of the problem. Is there a role for government spending and, if so, what are "good" government interventions?

Looking at the cross-country data in figure 4.1, we see a strong positive relationship between inequality as measured by the Gini coefficient and intergenerational persistence in income—more

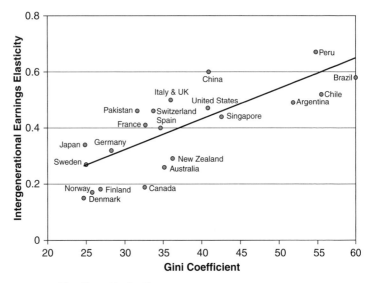

FIGURE 4.1. The Great Gatsby Curve

Notes: Figure shows the relationship between inequality, as measured by the Gini coefficient on the x-axis, and intergenerational persistence, as measured by the intergenerational earnings elasticity on the y-axis. Higher values indicate more inequality and more persistence, respectively.

Source: Miles Corak, "Inequality from Generation to Generation: The United States in Comparison," in *The Economics of Inequality, Poverty, and Discrimination in the 21st Century, vol. 1,* edited by Robert Rycroft (Santa Barbara, CA: Praeger, 2013)

popularly known as the "Great Gatsby Curve" (Krueger 2012). The US, Italy, and the United Kingdom, for instance, are countries with relatively high levels of inequality and low intergenerational mobility. By contrast, the Scandinavian countries feature high levels of mobility and much less inequality.

As figure 4.2 shows, there is also a strong positive correlation between the college earnings premium and intergenerational persistence in incomes. Compared with other countries, the US has a very large college earnings premium, but it also has a lot more persistence in incomes across generations.

Intriguingly, this graph would look very similar if, instead of the college premium, we were to plot government spending on

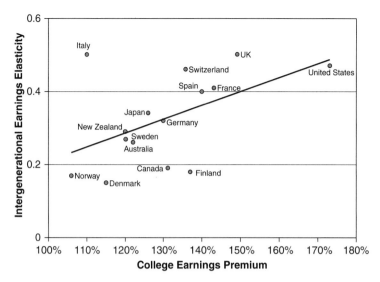

FIGURE 4.2. Intergenerational persistence and the college earnings premium

Notes: Figure shows the relationship between the college earnings premium (*x*-axis), as measured by the ratio of the average employment income of 25–34-year-old men with a college degree over that of their high-school educated counterparts, and intergenerational persistence (*y*-axis), as measured by the intergenerational earnings elasticity. Higher values indicate larger earnings premiums and more persistence, respectively.

Sources: Miles Corak, "Income Inequality, Equality of Opportunity, and Intergenerational Mobility," *Journal of Economic Perspectives* 27 (3); Miles Corak, "Inequality from Generation to Generation: The United States in Comparison," in *The Economics of Inequality, Poverty, and Discrimination in the 21st Century, vol. 1,* edited by Robert Rycroft (Santa Barbara, CA: Praeger, 2013); and OECD (2011)

tertiary education on the *x*-axis—i.e., government spending on higher education, elite universities, etc. The relationship would reverse, however, if one were to consider all government spending on education instead. This suggests that there is something about government spending on higher education (as opposed to government spending on primary education) that is correlated with intergenerational persistence.

Instead of looking across countries, let us look at intergenerational mobility within countries next. Figure 4.3 plots a son's probability of falling into a given earnings decile given that his father

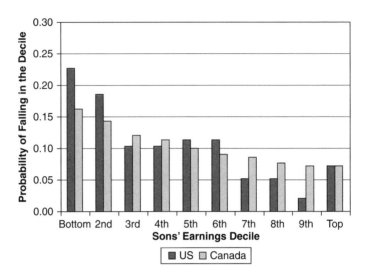

FIGURE 4.3. Earnings deciles of sons born to bottom-decile fathers

Notes: Figure shows the probability that a son whose father was in the first decile of the income distribution ends up in any given decile of his generation's distribution.

Sources: Miles Corak, "Income Inequality, Equality of Opportunity, and Intergenerational Mobility," *Journal of Economic Perspectives* 27 (3); Miles Corak and Andrew Heisz, "The Intergenerational Earnings and Income Mobility of Canadian Men: Evidence from Longitudinal Income Tax Data." *Journal of Human Resources* 34 (3) (1999); and Bhashkar Mazumder, "The Apple Falls Even Closer to the Tree than We Thought: New and Revised Estimates of the Intergenerational Inheritance of Earnings," in *Unequal Chances: Family Background and Economic Success,* ed. Samuel Bowles, Herbert Gintis, and Melissa Osborne Groves (New York: Russell Sage Foundation)

was in the bottom decile of the income distribution. It does so for both the US and Canada. For instance, if a US father was in the bottom decile of the income distribution of his generation, there is approximately a 22 percent probability that his son ends up in the bottom decile of the earnings distribution of the next generation. Strikingly, there is only about a 7 percent probability of the son falling in the top decile of the distribution. The same basic pattern holds in the US and Canada, although it is less pronounced in the latter. Loosely speaking, the data show that there is a lot of persistence at the bottom of the distribution. Simply put, children of poor parents are much more likely to end up being poor than rich.

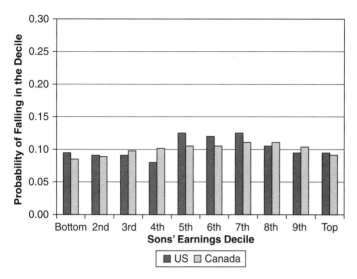

FIGURE 4.4. Earnings deciles of sons born to middle-two-decile fathers

Notes: Figure shows the probability that a son whose father was in either the fifth or the sixth decile of the income distribution ends up in any given decile of his generation's distribution.

Sources: Miles Corak and Andrew Heisz, "The Intergenerational Earnings and Income Mobility of Canadian Men: Evidence from Longitudinal Income Tax Data." *Journal of Human Resources* 34 (3) (1999); and Bhashkar Mazumder, "The Apple Falls Even Closer to the Tree than We Thought: New and Revised Estimates of the Intergenerational Inheritance of Earnings," in *Unequal Chances: Family Background and Economic Success,* ed. Samuel Bowles, Herbert Gintis, and Melissa Osborne Groves (New York: Russell Sage Foundation)

A very different picture emerges in figure 4.4, where, instead of conditioning on the father being in the bottom decile of the income distribution, we condition on him being in one of the two middle deciles. Although there is a weak tendency for the sons of these fathers to remain in the middle of the distribution, the probability of making it to the top—or the very bottom—is almost as high.

The last figure in this series, i.e., figure 4.5, deals with fathers in the top decile. Again, we see a lot of persistence, especially in the US. For instance, conditional on the father being in the top decile of the distribution, there is a 27 percent probability that the son will end up in the top decile as well.

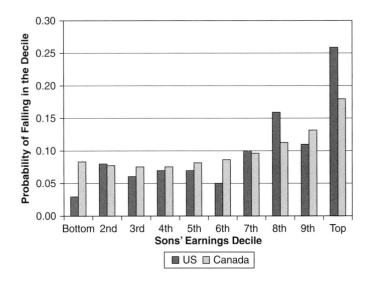

FIGURE 4.5. Earnings deciles of sons born to top-decile fathers

Notes: Figure shows the probability that a son whose father was in the tenth decile of the income distribution ends up in any given decile of his generation's distribution.

Sources: Miles Corak, "Income Inequality, Equality of Opportunity, and Intergenerational Mobility," *Journal of Economic Perspectives* 27 (3); Miles Corak and Andrew Heisz, "The Intergenerational Earnings and Income Mobility of Canadian Men: Evidence from Longitudinal Income Tax Data," *Journal of Human Resources* 34 (3) (1999); and Bhashkar Mazumder, "The Apple Falls Even Closer to the Tree than We Thought: New and Revised Estimates of the Intergenerational Inheritance of Earnings," in *Unequal Chances: Family Background and Economic Success,* ed. Samuel Bowles, Herbert Gintis, and Melissa Osborne Groves (New York: Russell Sage Foundation)

Why is there so much persistence at the top of the income distribution but not in the middle? Are there economic forces that imply high persistence in one part of the distribution but not in the other? One potential explanation is that rich parents invest a lot more in their children than poorer ones.

Figure 4.6 shows enrichment expenditures per child in the US. The data differentiate between parents with different incomes and are available for the period from 1972 to 2006. Even as early as the 1970s, there has always been a nontrivial difference in how much parents at opposite ends of the income distribution invest in their

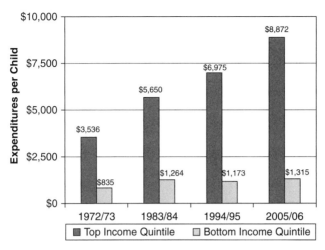

FIGURE 4.6. Enrichment expenditures per child in the US, by parental income

Notes: Numbers are in 2008 dollars and refer to parental spending on books, computers, child care, summer camps, private school, and other expenditures to promote children's abilities.

Sources: Miles Corak, "Income Inequality, Equality of Opportunity, and Intergenerational Mobility," *Journal of Economic Perspectives* 27 (3) (2013); and Greg Duncan and Richard Murnane, "Introduction: The American Dream, Then and Now," in *Whither Opportunity? Rising Inequality, Schools, and Children's Life Chances*, ed. Greg Duncan and Richard Murnane (New York: Russell Sage Foundation, 2011)

children. Perhaps more importantly, the gap has widened dramatically over the last three to four decades, and the same basic pattern holds not only for monetary expenditures, but also for parental time spent with children (see Guryan et al. 2008, Ramey and Ramey 2010). Guided by these facts, we develop a theory of the intergenerational transmission of resources. Our main goal is to understand why persistence among wealthy families is so much higher than in the middle class.

Our approach is simple yet powerful. Since labor income constitutes the vast majority of individuals' earnings—even among the "top 1 percent" (see Piketty and Saez 2003)—we believe that we have to understand inequality in human capital if we want to understand inequality within and across generations. In an attempt to do so, we model earnings (E) by assuming that each unit of human capital (H) yields a given rate of return (r), as in $E = rH + e$, where the random term e refers to all other determinants of earnings, such as market luck or macroeconomic conditions beyond individuals' control. Consistent with the empirical record, in our setup cross-sectional inequality increases directly with the return to education, i.e., r. Over the last three decades or so, the returns to education have risen dramatically, especially in the US (Juhn et al. 1993, Murphy and Katz 1992). At the same time, inequality has increased, as well.

Since education is the main determinant of earnings, intergenerational mobility in income depends critically on the persistence of human capital across generations. That is, how much of my own human capital is determined by the human capital or the earnings of my parents? All else equal, intergenerational mobility will be low whenever parents exert a great influence over their offspring's human capital.

Gary Becker's earlier work had already emphasized the importance of human capital for linking cross-sectional inequality and intergenerational mobility. Progress since, however, has been largely confined to empirical work (see Solon 1999 and Black and Devereux 2011 for useful reviews). We build on the early theoretical literature, but allow for complementarities in the "production" of human capital. That is, we allow more educated parents to be "better" at investing in the human capital of their children. This seemingly minor departure turns out to be very important. In fact, allowing for complementarities radically changes some of the existing literature's conclusions.

A simple formulation for the production of children's human capital is $H_c = F(y, H_p, G)$, where H_c denotes children's human capital, H_p is that of parents, y gives parental investments in children, and G is government spending. In words, we assume that children's human capital depends on the investments they receive from their parents, how educated their parents are, and how much the government spends on schools, etc. Naturally, all of these factors should have a positive effect on children's human capital.

The crucial assumption is that parental human capital and spending on children are complements. Technically, we posit that $\partial^2 H_c/\partial y \partial H_p > 0$. Essentially, this means that educated parents are more productive or more efficient at investing in their children. In this respect our analysis departs from previous work. Existing research has simply assumed that the productivity of parents' investments is independent of their own human capital.

Taking their human capital, i.e., H_p, and government spending, G, as given, parents choose how much to invest in their children. For analytic simplicity, I focus on the case with perfect capital markets, meaning that parents are not credit-constrained. When capital markets are perfect, even poor parents can invest as much as they want in the education of their children, say, by borrowing against the income of future generations. This does not imply that parents invest infinitely much. On the contrary, in the case of perfect capital markets, the return on investing in children has to be, at the margin, exactly as high as the return parents would get from putting their money or time to the next best use.

Of course, it is not clear whether the assumption of perfect capital markets is, in fact, satisfied. Much current research wrestles with precisely this question (see Lochner and Monge-Naranjo 2012 and the references therein). What makes this assumption attractive for our purposes is that it allows us to considerably simplify the analysis. Moreover, it brings out more starkly the difference between our results and those of previous work. Existing research generally concludes that perfect capital markets break the connection between parents' human capital and that of their children. The reason is that perfect capital markets allow *all* parents to invest the optimal amount in their children. Hence, equally able children will receive equal investments, independent of their parents' income, which, in turn, leads to similar levels of intergenerational mobility among children of the middle class and those of the rich. We have already seen that this is not true in the data, and our model explains why.

As a side note, we obtain broadly similar conclusions when we allow for lower-income families to be credit-constrained. The most important difference between the cases of perfect and imperfect capital markets is that credit constraints impose tight limits on how much poor parents can borrow and, therefore, invest in the human capital of their children. Thus, credit constraints directly lower the degree of intergenerational mobility at the bottom of the income distribution, as in figure 4.3. Since this is hardly surprising and since we are primarily interested in explaining why there is so much more persistence at the top of the distribution than among members of the middle class, we abstract from credit constraints—though we do pay careful attention to them in Becker et al. (2014).

If the return on savings is given by the economy-wide return on capital, R_k, then, at the optimum, the marginal return on investing in children's human capital must equal R_k. Or in symbols, $R_y \equiv rF_y = R_k$. This condition is, of course, familiar from Gary's seminal works on the economics of the family. The novel implication of our analysis is that high human capital parents invest more in children than their low human capital counterparts. The reason is simple: due to the assumed complementarities, investments of high human capital parents are more productive. Thus, highly educated parents invest more than their less educated counterparts.

After allowing for complementarities in the production function, even equally able children will receive different levels of investments from their parents, depending on whether the parents had high or low human capital. Not only does this prediction match the evidence in figure 4.6, it directly implies that children born into different families will end up in different parts of the income distribution.

By contrast, without complementarities in the production function, i.e., if parents' human capital had no effect on that of their offspring, equally able children would receive the same investments and, therefore, fall in the same part of the income distribution. In a world where the productivity of parental investments is independent of parental characteristics and other environmental factors, there would be perfect intergenerational mobility in income, at least conditional on ability. However, once we allow for complementarities—which we think are important in the real world—this conclusion breaks down.

Let us consider a closed-form example. Suppose that the production function for children's human capital is given by $H_c = \mu + \kappa y + \varphi y^2 + \theta y H_p + v_c$, where $\kappa, \theta > 0$ and $\varphi < 0$. In words, children's human capital depends positively on the investments they receive from their parents (y) as well as other factors that are beyond agents' control (v_c). Investments in children are subject to diminishing marginal returns but complementary to parental human capital (because $\theta > 0$).

Given these simplifying assumptions, it is straightforward to derive the optimal level of parental investments, i.e., $y^* = (R_k/r - \kappa - \theta y H_p)/(2\varphi)$. We use this expression to obtain a reduced-form relationship between the human capital of children and that of their parents: $H_c = \mu^* + \delta^* H_p + \gamma^* H_p^2 + v_c$, where $\mu^* \equiv \mu - (\kappa^2 r^2 - R_k^2)/(4 \varphi r^2)$, $\delta^* \equiv -(\kappa\theta)/(2\varphi)$, $\gamma^* \equiv -(\kappa\theta)/(4\varphi)$. The fact that the relationship between children's and parent's human capital is quadratic turns out to be important.

Why? A convex relationship implies that the influence of parents' human capital on that of their children increases as parents become more educated. Mathematically, $\partial^2 H_c/\partial H_p^2 > 0$. That is, not only will children of more educated parents be more educated themselves, but the marginal impact of additional parental human capital rises. Hence, children born to parents in the upper part of the income distribution will be more similar to their parents (in terms of human capital) than children born to caregivers in the lower part of the distribution, which implies greater intergenerational persistence at the top.

While the example above may seem quite stylized, our conclusions hold much more generally. Unless there are strong diminishing marginal returns to parental human capital, complementarity in the production function implies more persistence at the top. Particular to the example is that the degree of persistence in human capital, and therefore the degree of intergenerational mobility, does not depend on the market return of human capital, i.e., r. In more general formulations, the effect of a rise in the return to education can go either way. That is, it can either lower or increase the degree of intergenerational persistence.

The media often convey the impression that increases in the market return to human capital lower mobility. Our analysis shows that need not be the case. Although rising returns to human capital aggravate the consequences of the birth lottery (because the income distribution spreads out), they do not necessarily change the intergenerational transmission of human capital itself. Measuring intergenerational mobility with respect to individuals' position in their generation's income distribution, our model predicts almost no change over the last few decades—despite the large increase in the college premium. Perhaps surprisingly, this prediction is supported by the best (newly) available empirical evidence (see Chetty et al. 2014).

To think about steady states and the long-run distribution of human capital, let us go back to the example. Figure 4.7 depicts the relationship between children's human capital (on the y-axis) and that of their parents (on the x-axis). In panel A on the top left, we analyze the usual case, in which there is only one steady state. In

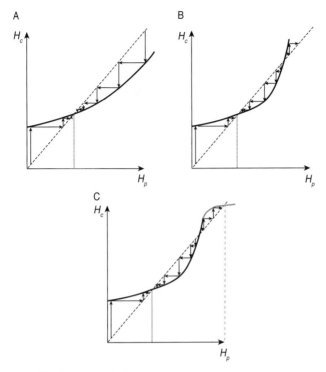

FIGURE 4.7. Steady state analysis

Source: Author's illustration

this panel, the transmission function crosses the forty-five-degree line from above. Thus, the steady state is stable; and over the long run, there is strong regression to the population mean.

In our model, however, this is not the only possible case. Panel B on the top right depicts a scenario in which complementarities in the production of children's human capital are so strong that the transmission function crosses the forty-five-degree line twice—first from above and then from below. Economically, this means that children of very highly educated parents end up having even more human capital than the previous generation. As a consequence, there is bifurcation. One set of families regresses toward the mean, whereas an "elite" keeps regressing away from the mean.

Naturally, unbounded regression away from the mean is not necessarily realistic. It seems reasonable that, at some point, even the elite's human capital would level out. To incorporate this feature we can add a small cubic term to the transmission function in Panel C. The result is a second stable steady state. There would thus be a highly persistent elite atop the distribution (i.e., around the stable steady state featuring high human capital) as well as a persistent "underclass" at the bottom (i.e., around the stable steady state featuring low human capital). Among the middle class, however, there would be a lot of churning—especially as the point where the transmission function crosses the forty-five-degree line from below constitutes an unstable steady state. Our model can, therefore, rationalize why there seems to be a lot of persistence at both ends of the income distribution. Importantly, there need not be any credit constraints for this to be true.

Before concluding, I will briefly discuss the role of government spending. To incorporate government spending into our analysis, we let G enter the production function for children's human capital. We assume that, all else equal, government spending weakly raises the human capital of children—simply because well-intentioned governments are probably not doing any direct harm. That does not mean, however, that there are no unintended side effects. The reason is that other factors are not necessarily going to be equal. When parental inputs adjust in response to government interventions, the key question becomes: how do G, y, and H_p interact?

We analyze two cases, which together cover a wide range of real-world government programs. In the first case, government spending (G) and parental investments (y) are perfect substitutes. For instance, if the government provides school books for children, parents are unlikely to incur the same expense. A similar argument may apply to, say, computers, free lunches, and a number of other educational supplies. Of course, if government spending is a perfect substitute for spending by parents, then private spending is going to be crowded out one for one. Total investments in children's human capital will only increase if the government spends more than parents would.

Given that parental investments were optimal to begin with (due to the assumption of perfect capital markets), this gives rise to an important equity-efficiency trade-off. If crowding out is quantitatively important, then government interventions that increase the human-capital acquisition of children have to be very large, which raises concerns about the deadweight loss of taxation. Moreover, the marginal return on this spending is (weakly) lower than the return on capital. For this kind of intervention to be justified, a social planner would have to put a lot of weight on equity.

At least in part, the welfare effect of government interventions will depend on whether families are credit-constrained. In the presence of credit constraints, human-capital investments among poor families are not optimal. Thus, interventions that raise total spending on the children of these families may actually be welfare-improving. In particular, if the deadweight loss of taxation is not too high, there may not be an equity-efficiency trade-off at all. By contrast, if capital markets are perfect, that is, when parental investments are (close to) optimal, then there is little role for government spending.

As a side note, there is no consensus (yet) as to how important credit constraints are (for opposing results, see, for instance, Lovenheim 2011, Carneiro and Heckman 2002, or Belley and Lochner 2007). One strand of the literature finds that, conditional on a host of observables, parental resources and children's educational attainment are almost uncorrelated. These studies argue that credit constraints cannot be quantitatively important. Another set of studies does find a positive correlation, especially in recent years, which is then interpreted as evidence of credit constraints. Our analysis implies that such tests are theoretically ill-founded.

As we have seen earlier, even in a world with perfect capital markets, if there are complementarities in production, then children's human capital will generally be correlated with that of their parents and, therefore, with parental income.

Next, we analyze the (perhaps more interesting) case in which government spending and private investments are complements. Under this assumption, additional government spending increases the productivity of parental investments, which in turn induces families to invest more. Examples where such multiplier effects are plausible might include government spending on better teachers or elite universities.

Even when government spending does not crowd out private investments, there is still an equity-efficiency trade-off, though of a different kind. To clearly bring out this trade-off, consider a government that spends an equal amount of money on children in rich and poor families. Although such a government program may seem neutral, its effects are not. Government interventions of this kind actually *increase* inequality.

Why? The reason is that when government spending and private investments are complements, then additional government funds will have a bigger impact on the human capital of children in rich families. After all, their parents have more human capital, making the government spending more productive. Again, this result is a direct consequence of complementarities in the production function. Moreover, higher human capital families increase their own investments in children because these investments are being made more productive by the government intervention. To be just "neutral" in the sense of raising the human capital of all children equally, government spending would have to be biased toward poor families.

This, however, raises efficiency concerns. When capital markets are perfect, poor families are the ones in which additional government spending is the *least* productive. The efficient use of funds in this case would be to invest in the children of rich families. Yet, from the perspective of a social planner who is also concerned about equity, that may be undesirable.

Again, these conclusions are greatly altered if credit constraints limit poor families' ability to optimally invest in their children. If credit constraints are sufficiently important, then biasing government spending toward children in poor families may be equity-*and* efficiency-enhancing.

To conclude, our analysis builds on earlier theoretical work that links human capital to intergenerational mobility and cross-sectional inequality. We depart from the existing literature by emphasizing complementarities in the production of children's human capital. If these complementarities are sufficiently strong, our theory predicts lower intergenerational mobility at the top of the income distribution than in the middle—even in the absence of credit constraints.

Moreover, our analysis implies that well-intentioned government policies may end up having perverse consequences, depending on whether a particular intervention is a substitute or complement to private spending. In reality, many government programs likely have elements of both, which makes predicting their effect even harder.

Beyond what I have already mentioned, our model is useful for thinking about the likely consequences of many recent changes in the marketplace. For instance, not only has the US experienced a dramatic increase in the returns to education, but assortative mating has become more important as well. The probability that a college-educated man marries a college-educated woman is much higher today than it was forty years ago. Suitably extended, our theory implies that such changes result in less regression to the mean in ability and, therefore, in less intergenerational mobility. A number of other extensions and implications are explained in our working paper (see Becker et al. 2014).

Question and Answer Session

QUESTION: *If we take to heart your interpretation of the facts, it seems to me it becomes quite important for researchers to unpack the sources of complementarity in the production of children's human capital. Another way to put the issue is: what is it about higher levels of human capital that shifts up the schedule that describes the return of parental investment in children's human capital? Is it something as simple as reading a bedtime story to a four-year-old, which is a skill that might be easily transmitted to many people? Or is it something that requires the kind of vocabulary and thinking process that comes along with a college education, which is obviously a much more costly thing to transmit?*

And the answer to that question, it seems to me, also has profound implications for the proper role of government, if government sets it as a goal to reduce inequality, about how to do it. It may be that if there are simple methods of teaching parents with lower levels of human capital, what are the skills, what are the habits, what are the practices that increase the returns on their investments in their children, that maybe government policy ought to be directed in that way.

SPENKUCH: I agree with you, and I wish that I knew the exact source of these complementarities. As you said, there are certain tasks, like reading a bedtime story, that parents can do about equally well—at least parents with a minimal level of human capital. But once we think about tasks that require just a little more education, complementarities may start to become important. For instance, it is easy for you to help your son with his algebra homework, but if his parents were high school dropouts or GED graduates instead, that might not be the case anymore. Such parents may be able to spend a lot of time with their children, but each unit of time is likely less effective than if they were more educated.

QUESTION: *I'd like to complicate your problem by describing California. For many students, the government has a monopoly over access to education. The government spending produces the public school and you have to go to it. You don't have a choice. They're trying to expand choice, but the reality is, for many students, they have no choice. The teachers in the school are unionized and their dues are deducted automatically from their paycheck. The teachers' union has a gigantic cash flow, which they spend in elections. And they elect the people who they then bargain with or who control the schools. That puts you in an odd position. And there's been an interesting lawsuit in LA, which is catching attention, where California was sued for violating the Constitution and depriving kids of a decent education because of refusal to fire incompetent teachers. According to the rules, it's practically impossible to get rid of somebody. Now the governor and the attorney general are both going to contest this ruling by arguing that incompetent teachers have a constitutional right to ruin kids' lives. It's going to be wonderful to see how this plays itself out.*

SPENKUCH: Let me play devil's advocate—just for a little bit. As devil's advocate, I would argue that the government is really effective at reducing inequality. If everybody gets the same poor education, everybody ends up poor. Of course, this is not prudent policy. Linking your question to the model, our analysis would say, since the government provides only a deficient education, it is important to figure out what parents do in addition to that. For instance, you might imagine that many high-socioeconomic-status parents purchase, say, SAT tutoring for their children, or piano and violin lessons. Those are enrichment expenditures that governments typically do not provide.

Comment: *There's this implicit assumption that the government provides it. Maybe they spend equal dollars on everybody, and that's an equal education. The truth is the well-educated parents are much better at navigating the system both within a district and across districts. Talk to anybody who does special education and they know that the well-educated parents are in there arguing for every little thing their child is entitled to that's within a district, let alone the fact that they move to districts where the public schooling actually is pretty good.*

So the idea that the government is giving everybody an equal deal and that education matters less when the government's providing it doesn't seem to be consistent with the facts. Wal-Mart is more similar in poor and rich neighborhoods than schools are. I always think that's a great comparison to make. I walk into my Wal-Mart, and it looks a lot like the Wal-Mart in another neighborhood that's a lot poorer, but the schools don't look anything like each other.

It's interesting because one of the big equalizers for people is the market. People get to take advantage of other people's skills. And when you do education in this way, you defeat that market mechanism. I can't use the skills of other people to help educate my kids. I've got to do it myself. I've got to know where to live, I've got to know how to navigate the system, how to get the best teachers, all of those things. It's actually raising inequality. And this fits into what Jörg was talking about earlier. How is this government spending really a complement or a substitute?

One of the things that happens in the market is you get all these changes and there's increasing demand for more skilled workers, but there's a supply response that benefits everybody, including those who aren't so educated, because they get to take advantage of what doesn't happen in a household. You're much more on your own in a household and that's why this complementarity is so important, and why government spending, by defeating the market in many ways, actually makes it worse rather than better.

QUESTION: *One question and two observations. On figures 4.3 to 4.5, you have the sons in particular deciles. That has to be at a point in time. So as you're laying that out, I'm wondering what point in time. People move between deciles a lot and so I'd just like one answer, if you'd hold it for the other two.*

And what I find striking in the twenty-first century, even late twentieth century, is just looking at sons. I mean, there are daughters, right? Anyway, that's quite striking to me.

The other thing that strikes me is that your whole model is based on the idea that human capital is like other capital and there's not a big signaling element. If you have a big signaling element—I'm a blogger at EconLog with Bryan Caplan, he's writing a book on this. And he finds that signaling—he's already got a lot of data—signaling is huge. It's probably well over half. And what you're going to do is just have more rats running around the wheel if you put more money into it.

SPENKUCH: I completely agree with your last point, there may very well be signaling. If you wanted to incorporate signaling into the model, you could allow for parents who went to, say, Harvard to have an easier time getting their children into other elite universities. The model is actually quite flexible. It depends on what you want to call "human capital." Broadly construed, human capital might include all personal characteristics that raise wages. As long as there is still a complementarity between those characteristics and investments in children's human capital, our conclusions continue to go through.

To your earlier point about sons and daughters, there is an emerging literature that looks at the earnings of daughters and how they correlate with those of their parents. Econometrically, such an exercise is a lot harder to do than the corresponding one for sons because of selection into market work. Even in the twenty-first century, not all daughters work, and the ones who do are probably systematically different from the ones who do not. This may be the reason for why, even today, most of the literature focuses on sons.

Coming back to your very first point about how these graphs are constructed: the papers on which these graphs are based average earnings over a period of time, sometimes ten years or even longer. Ideally, one would like to look at lifetime earnings, but the available data now do not allow for that yet.

QUESTION: *I really like the paper and started thinking through some of the implications. And you touched on the credit constraints but I would use a different terminology. I would say tests for whether parental income matters for kids' investments holding kids' ability constant—put it that way because that's the only way to make sense in your model.*

My question for you is: if those tests fail, isn't that a rejection of your technology? And then the next thing I wanted to point out about credit constraints is that consumption data is very helpful. Even in your technology, I believe the consumption data is going to reveal—or fail to reveal—credit constraints. And it also solves your sons-and-daughters problem because maybe all daughters don't work but they all consume. And there's data on consumption. People have used it to look at these mobility issues. And so I think you can promote that literature a little bit.

SPENKUCH: I completely agree with you. Ultimately, people derive utility from consumption, and we should look at that. Regarding the earlier point: our model predicts a positive correlation between parental resources and the education of children, even after controlling for ability. The reason is that there are complementarities in production. The previous literature has interpreted these correlations as evidence of credit constraints. We, however, argue that such a conclusion is premature, at least if we think that complementarities are quantitatively important.

QUESTION: *Seems to me that today there are two classes of people, say, graduating from a Stanford or a prestigious university—those who have no debt because their parents have been able to pay for everything and those who come out, however bright and well-educated, they're way down in a hole. So if you're looking at their future income possibilities and so forth, in one case, people can't save at an earlier age and invest and complement their income, whereas others can, if they're wisely guided. They'll be able to start investing at a much earlier age. There's been an accumulation of huge amounts of student debt. How is that going to play into this? And to what extent is that debt, since a lot of it isn't going to get repaid, essentially a government subsidy?*

SPENKUCH: Your point about student debt strikes me as very important. Most research is concerned with correlations in incomes or positions in the income distribution, but we fail to look at lifetime utility. It is quite plausible that someone who graduated from Stanford with a hundred and fifty thousand dollars of debt has much lower lifetime utility than someone else who is otherwise similar but does not have as much debt. If we could look at lifetime utility, we would probably find that parental resources have a much greater effect on utility than on educational attainment or salaries.

References

Becker, Gary, Kevin Murphy, Scott Kominers, and Jörg Spenkuch. 2014. "A Theory of Intergenerational Mobility," mimeographed, University of Chicago.

Becker, Gary, and Nigel Tomes. 1979. "An Equilibrium Theory of the Distribution of Income and Intergenerational Mobility." *Journal of Political Economy* 87 (6): 1153–1189.

Becker, Gary, and Nigel Tomes. 1986. "Human Capital and the Rise and Fall of Families." *Journal of Labor Economics* 4 (3): S1–S39.

Belley, Philippe, and Lance Lochner. 2007. "The Changing Role of Family Income and Ability in Determining Educational Achievement." *Journal of Human Capital* 1 (1): 37–89.

Black, Sandra, and Paul Devereux. 2011. "Recent Developments in Intergenerational Mobility." In *Handbook of Labor Economics, vol. 4B,* edited by David Card and Orley C. Ashenfelter, 1487–1541. San Diego, CA: North Holland.

Carneiro, Pedro, and James Heckman. 2002. "The Evidence on Credit Constraints in Post-Secondary Schooling." *Economic Journal* 112 (482): 705–734.

Chetty, Raj, Nathaniel Hendren, Patrick Kline, Emmanuel Saez, and Nicholas Turner. 2014. "Is the United States Still a Land of Opportunity? Recent Trends in Intergenerational Mobility." NBER Working Paper No. 19844.

Corak, Miles. 2013a. "Income Inequality, Equality of Opportunity, and Intergenerational Mobility." *Journal of Economic Perspectives* 27 (3): 79–102.

Corak, Miles. 2013b. "Inequality from Generation to Generation: The United States in Comparison." In *The Economics of Inequality, Poverty, and Discrimination in the 21st Century, vol. 1,* edited by Robert Rycroft. Santa Barbara, CA: Praeger.

Corak, Miles, and Andrew Heisz. 1999. "The Intergenerational Earnings and Income Mobility of Canadian Men: Evidence from Longitudinal Income Tax Data." *Journal of Human Resources* 34 (3): 504–533.

Duncan, Greg, and Richard Murnane. 2011. "Introduction: The American Dream, Then and Now," in *Whither Opportunity? Rising Inequality, Schools, and Children's Life Chances*, edited by Greg Duncan and Richard Murnane. New York: Russell Sage Foundation.

Guryan, Jonathan, Erik Hurst, and Melissa Kearney. 2008. "Parental Education and Parental Time with Children." *Journal of Economic Perspectives* 22 (3): 23–46.

Juhn, Chinhui, Kevin Murphy, and Brooks Pierce. 1993. "Wage Inequality and the Rise in the Returns to Skill." *Journal of Political Economy* 101 (3): 410–442.

Krueger, Alan. 2012. "The Rise and Consequences of Inequality in the United States." Speech at the Center for American Progress, Washington, DC.

Lochner, Lance, and Alexander Monge-Naranjo. 2012. "Credit Constraints in Education." *Annual Review of Economics* 4 (1): 225–256.

Lovenheim, Michael. 2011. "The Effect of Liquid Housing Wealth on College Enrollment." *Journal of Labor Economics* 29 (4): 741–777.

Mazumder, Bhashkar. 2005. "The Apple Falls Even Closer to the Tree than We Thought: New and Revised Estimates of the Intergenerational Inheritance of Earnings," in *Unequal Chances: Family Background and Economic Success,* edited by Samuel Bowles, Herbert Gintis, and Melissa Osborne Groves. New York: Russell Sage Foundation.

Murphy, Kevin, and Lawrence Katz. 1992. "Changes in Relative Wages, 1963–1987: Supply and Demand Factors." *Quarterly Journal of Economics* 107 (1): 35–78.

OECD. 2011. *Education at a Glance 2011: OECD Indicators*. Paris: OECD Publishing.

Piketty, Thomas, and Emmanuel Saez. 2003. "Income Inequality in the United Sates, 1913–1998." *Quarterly Journal of Economics* 118 (1): 1–39.

Ramey, Valerie, and Garey Ramey. 2010. "The Rug Rat Race." *Brookings Papers on Economic Activity,* Spring 2010: 129–176.

Solon, Gary. 1999. "Intergenerational Mobility in the Labor Market." In *Handbook of Labor Economics, vol. 3A,* edited by David Card and Orley C. Ashenfelter. Amsterdam: Elsevier.

CHAPTER FIVE

The Effects of Redistribution Policies on Growth and Employment

Casey B. Mulligan

I'll start with a two-sentence summary, so you can get right to the weaknesses of what I'm going to say. First sentence: the federal government has recently created or expanded a number of redistribution programs, and these programs have made the American economy smaller than it would have been. Second sentence: the effects of these programs are right in line with basic economics, right in line with basic price theory, but the opposite of what the program advocates have been telling us. So a natural reaction, I think, to those two sentences would be—and this is kind of an early Milton Friedman style of conclusion—would be to say, "Hey, these policies are bad ideas. We're not sure where they came from. And they could have been rectified by giving some combination of voters, politicians, and bureaucrats a better economic education." In short, if everybody just studied price theory, what a wonderful world it would be.

And I'm not sure I'm going to be able to tell you more than that today.

But I know that Gary Becker would have pushed back on that. And he did push back when we had working groups on these topics. He would push back and say, "Wait a second. Don't side with the guy on the left in this picture [Milton Friedman]. The guy on the right [George Stigler] had some things to say, too." And he would say, "You can do all the educating you want, and there are still going to be the fundamental economic and political forces pushing for these policies."

Milton Friedman (left) walking with fellow University of Chicago economist George Stigler.

I don't know what these fundamental forces are. I'm just going to tell you what the results are in terms of policy.

Now let's talk about redistribution policy. There's an excess of attention on the personal income tax. I'll start with figure 5.1 of marginal tax rates as calculated by NBER [National Bureau of Economic Research] for the personal income taxes at the federal and state levels. Each tick in this graph is two points, so the last several years here you don't see a lot of action. The moves in this tax are in the tenths of percentage points. Basically, this tax hasn't changed.

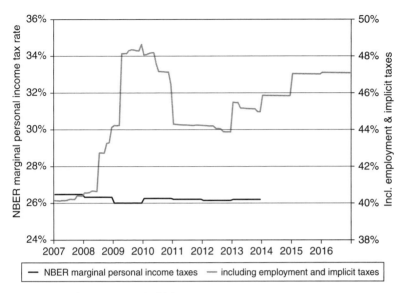

FIGURE 5.1. Statutory marginal labor tax rates
Source: National Bureau of Economic Research.

And if you focus on personal income taxes too much, then you say we haven't really changed the redistribution we've been doing.

Now, there are a couple problems with this graph the way I've drawn it here. It doesn't have employment taxes. And I think if you're interested in employment, of course income taxes are relevant. People have jobs to earn income. But also, employment taxes are relevant for employment.

The gray lines include those implicit income taxes into the picture. Each tick is still two points. The levels are different, but now we have a lot more happening. And I want to tell you some of the story behind what is happening.

I tried to organize some of the policy changes in table 5.1 by time period and by type of tax. Employment tax is the one that gets the least attention. That's in the first column. In the second column are the income taxes. In the interest of time, I'm going to jump to the middle period of 2007 to 2013, where there is a lot of legislative action

TABLE 5.1. New employment and income taxes in recent history

Explicit taxes are indicated in italics; all other taxes are implicit taxes

Time period	Employment taxes	Income Taxes

before 2007	Disability expansions
	    esp., wider range of ailments
		Medicaid expansions
		    Eligibility, esp. children
		    Growing market value of free
		    health insurance

2007–2013	Work requirements dropped
	UI expansions
	    more weeks of eligibility
	    other eligibility expansions
	    benefit increases
	Unemployment-tested assistance
	    with health insurance
	3 Federal minimum wage
	    increases
		Food stamps expansions
		    eligibility
		    benefit increases
		Means-tested loan forgiveness
		    mortgages
		    student loans

2014–2016	ACA HI assistance *ACA employer penalty*	ACA HI assistance ACA Medicaid expansions *AGA Medicare tax surcharges*

Source: Author's summary

in both employment and income taxes. You probably heard of the infamous ninety-nine weeks of unemployment insurance. That's one of the items here. But there are a bunch of items here that have little to do with ninety-nine weeks of unemployment insurance. There were a lot of new employment taxes that never made the newspaper.

Each one of these is a fascinating story. But I picked out two as a representative picture from the population. So I'll talk about some of the unemployment-tested health insurance and some of the food stamp expansions. The period from 2014–2016 is interesting in its own way, because these are all policies that come with the Affordable Care Act. There are a number of different aspects of that, and I'll tell you about some of these. And then in italics, I've indicated that only two of these taxes are explicit taxes that a politician would actually call a tax. The rest of them are implicit.

The first employment tax I will tell you about is the subsidy for

COBRA policies. COBRA refers to a long-standing law allowing people to continue participation in their former employer's health plan. Traditionally, that was an expensive proposition for the individual. You left your employer and stayed in the plan, but you had to pay for everything. Your employer probably wasn't going to be paying anymore. And you had to do it with after-tax dollars. So it was pretty expensive, and there were a lot of good reasons why people would avoid being laid off or try to avoid quitting. If they were laid off or quit, there was an incentive to hurry back to work. Well, the so-called stimulus law, the ARRA [American Recovery and Reinvestment Act of 2009], totally reversed that calculus. If you were laid off from your job and you liked your former employer health plan, you could keep it. And the federal government would pay about two-thirds. Now the scales were reversed, so that the cheaper way to get insurance would actually be to be off the job, rather than on the job. And this is a pretty big deal, not only because of the number of people—about two million workers plus dependents—who took part in this, but also it was kind of a preview to the real film that's coming, which was the Affordable Care Act. It was kind of a test run of the Affordable Care Act, as we will see.

The second one I want to tell you about is now called SNAP [Supplemental Nutrition Assistance Program], although it is known colloquially as food stamps. Food stamps are a combination of a tax on income, a tax on assets, and a subsidy from employment, all in the same bundle. Traditionally, that's the way it worked. One thing that happened in 2008 was that they cut the asset tax. So that put more people in a situation where they're paying an income tax rather than an asset tax. The other thing that happened was they got rid of the work requirement (or the employment subsidy if you think of it that way), so two things at the same time created a new income tax and a new employment tax for people, relative to the baseline.

Basically, SNAP has become a kind of unemployment insurance for unmarried people. There's no limit. You can be on there more than ninety-nine weeks. And really the only restriction, so to speak, is it's hard to be on there if you're married. Here's a statistic I have from fiscal year 2010. In a typical week, about 85 percent of unemployed, unmarried, non-elderly household heads were in food stamp households. And I'm not just picking some tiny little population with only a few people in it. The numerator of that 85 percent is over three million people. So this is a kind of new unemployment program, it is ongoing. The only temporary part was some benefit bonus they put on there, but all the rest continues, and there's no schedule to changing any of it.

That's the middle busy period from 2007 to 2013. The next period has to do with the Affordable Care Act. There are a lot of taxes in there and I don't have time to tell you all about them. But I'm going to tell you about my two favorites. And to introduce you to those, I need to tell you about some of the components in that big, complicated law that are related to health insurance coverage. The number one component is the market exchanges. They're exchanges where people can buy health insurance, and it is often subsidized in a couple of different ways. The second part is the employer mandate, that's enforced with the penalty that I'm going to tell you about. There are two other parts I'm not going to talk about much today, which are the individual mandate and the Medicaid expansions, but I'm going to focus on the first two.

In those marketplaces, there are two taxes that are large and many small ones. There are two that often get mixed together, but they are economically distinct. And the second part, the employer penalty, is actually a lot more significant than it first appears. I'll explain to you why—when you first look at it—you're only seeing a tip of the iceberg there.

Let's start with the employer penalty. That is a penalty that is important to understand. It only applies to full-time employees, and only when they are on the payroll. If you are unemployed, no one is penalizing you or penalizing an employer on your behalf. That is pretty important to the economics. It's indexed to health insurance costs, so it's probably going to grow faster than wages and faster than the economy into the future. It disproportionally hits low-skilled workers. Imagine that I kept talking to you guys today until dark, and then I kept going for a couple more hours. That's how many hours minimum-wage workers have to work so their employer can pay this penalty. That's a long time. Every week, they have to work eight hours to pay off that penalty. One reason why it's so many hours is that, unlike salaries, these penalties are not deductible from business taxes. So you've heard the penalty probably referred to as the $2,000 penalty, but in reality it is a $3,000 penalty if you look at it in terms of a salary equivalent. So for a minimum-wage worker, that is a lot of money on an annual basis. Also, it has anti-competitive aspects. I'm referring to competition in the labor market. Small employers don't pay this penalty. And you might hope, as a fan of markets, that there would be some competition, that the low-penalty players in the market could out-compete the high-penalty players. The problem is, if they try to out-compete the high-penalty players, they become high-penalty players themselves. There's a tremendous penalty—over $60,000 annually—for going over the threshold between small and large employers. So I think you're in a situation where you're going to have not only a penalty that's going to be paid by some employers, but you have the anti-competitive effects.

Now let's talk about the health insurance marketplaces. Figure 5.2 shows income on the horizontal axis and payments for health care on the vertical axis. The horizontal line represents paying full price for health care, which means it's independent of your income. Whatever your health care is, you pay, whether you're rich or you're poor. I've drawn another line for a discount, but the same discount for everybody. So that's why it's another horizontal line, but it's lower because it's a discount. What the Affordable Care Act

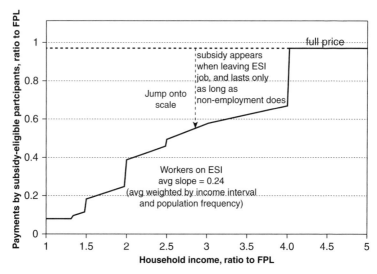

FIGURE 5.2. Health insurance marketplaces
Source: Author's calculations

says is, if you want to have the discount, you cannot be a full-time worker at an employer that offers coverage—which of course is most employees. This is a kind of full-time employment tax, and that's what the arrow is showing. You can't get that discount unless you leave that full-time position somehow, either to part-time work, or unemployment, or you're out of the labor force, making it a full-time employment tax.

I'm over-simplifying here, because the discount line is not really a horizontal line in the real law. It's an upward sloping line. And because it's an upward sloping line, it's also an income tax. But I want to emphasize that the full-time employment tax has not disappeared. When I've gone from my simple example to the real law, that arrow is still there. So not only is there a penalty on earning income as you move up and down the solid line, but there's also a penalty for being employed, and those are distinct economically, and you've got to look at them both. The slope, by the way, of the solid line . . . it's got a lot of slopes, but it averages about twenty-four. That's not a trivial thing. That's on top of all the other taxes that people pay.

Figure 5.3 is a summary of my three favorite taxes in the law. The black lines are telling us about the percentage of people who experience this tax. When I say "experience it," I don't mean pay it. I mean it's in their budget set. Whether they pay it or not is a choice, which is an analysis we do once we determine how large these taxes are. And then the gray bars are indicating how large the tax is, from the point of view of the people who are sitting in the black bars. And these are big numbers. Each tick on the side here is five percentage points. A number of these taxes look like almost doubling the payroll tax from employer and employee among the people who would be experiencing them.

Now I want to show you some behavioral analysis of these taxes. I'm going to start at an aggregate level. Having three groups is not aggregate enough for me, so I'm going to multiply the gray and the

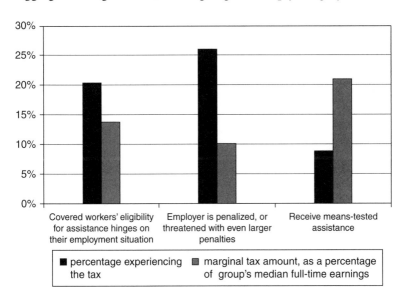

FIGURE 5.3. Taxes in Affordable Care Act

Source: Mulligan, Casey B., *Side Effects and Complications* (Chicago: University of Chicago Press, 2015.)

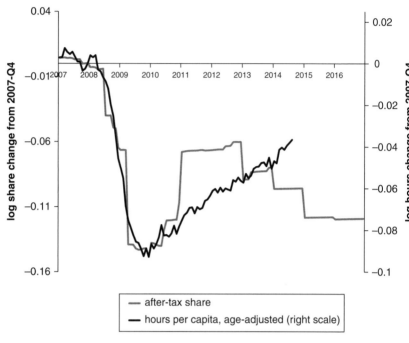

FIGURE 5.4. Safety net rules compared with work hours
Source: Author's calculations

black together, make an index, and use fixed population rates to redo that index every month. And I'm going to not only include the Affordable Care Act's new taxes, but all the new taxes that are displayed on table 5.1. I flipped it upside down to represent not what you pay when you earn more, but what you keep. And I've also put it on a log scale. That's the after-tax share. Here's where we are today. And then I'm going to plot labor market performance by measuring work hours per person, adjusted for the average age of the population. The work hours are in black. These are not exactly on the same scale. I'm not sure I'd want to use an elasticity of one to connect these two together, which is what you'd be doing if you put them on a common scale. Taxes went down, and the market went down. When the labor market came back somewhat, taxes came back somewhat.

Here's another way to look at what has happened. Figure 5.5 shows measures of wages. Of course, I think in terms of supply and demand. That's what Gary taught me. But there's a supply price and a demand price, and I'm showing you both in the labor market. I'm showing you employer costs, the demand price for labor in the black, and I'm showing you the supply price, the employee reward to working after all the taxes and subsidies. Starting with the black line, I think it went up somewhat. What's important to me is that you look at it on this scale. Namely, when you're looking at employer costs, look at it on the same scale that you use to look at the employee reward. You have room to fit the 12 percent drop in the employee reward to working that happened during this period. We can argue what has happened to employer costs, and maybe they went down, but it's nothing like what happened to the employee reward to work. It took a very big hit and remains quite low.

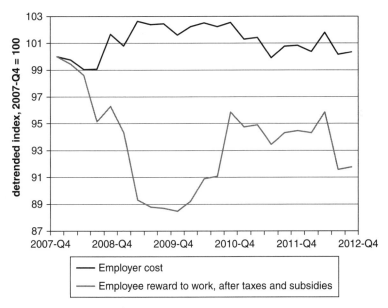

FIGURE 5.5. Measures of wages

Source: Author's calculations

Next I'll show you some cross-sectional behavioral patterns. I'm going to do this kind of tax rate analysis separately for ten groups. There are five groups based on skill, and each of the skill groups are broken into married and unmarried. I'm going to do a tax rate for each of the ten groups, and then I'm going to do an hours change. I'm going to do a gray series for each of the groups and a black series, and then I'm going to put them into a scatter plot.

The incentives will be on the bottom, and so farther to the right will mean a greater increase in incentives for working. Changes in hours worked from 2007 to 2010 are on the vertical axis.

Figure 5.6 shows married groups in black and unmarried groups in gray. The labels show you for these groups what they typically earn per month when they work full-time. Often you hear that in a recession, the low-skill groups are hit the hardest. You don't really see that among the married people. They all went down around 6 percent except for the most skilled group. Also, maybe it's just a coincidence that their incentives measured this way also went down about the same amount, about twelve log points.

Now let me show you the unmarried people. They don't all bunch together, either in their incentives or in their hours worked changes, except the bottom two groups. Those two have more or less the same hours changes and incentives changes. So maybe it is too naïve, but basic economics says, "Well, you'd expect the groups that have their incentives lowered the most would be the ones with hours that decline the most." And you see what you'd expect.

It's not true that taxes have been constant in these years. Broadly measured to include employment taxes and implicit taxes, they've gone up quite a bit. Incentives have been eroded because there's more redistribution than there was a few years ago. That redistribution has reduced the return to working quite a bit, and it should remain low if the laws on the books stay on the books.

The laws that created these new taxes were called stimulus laws, but by taxing employment and income, you get less employment

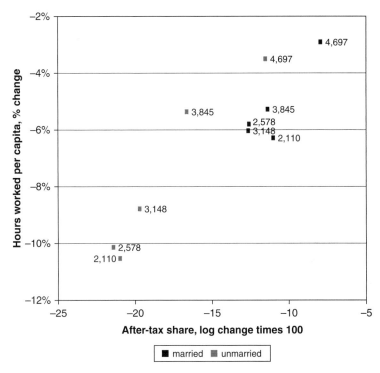

FIGURE 5.6. Full-time wages for married and unmarried workers

Source: Mulligan, Casey B., "Recent Marginal Labor Income Tax Rate Changes by Skill and Marital Status." *Tax Policy and the Economy* 27 (2013): 69–100

and less income. My estimates suggest it about doubled the size of the contraction measured in terms of average work hours. On a permanent basis, about half of potential workers will have a major new disincentive going forward in their budget set as a consequence of the health law. I estimate that employment and aggregate hours are going to be reduced by 3 percent due to the health law, and national income reduced by 2 percent due to the health law.

Let me go back and make the case for economic education versus politics. The first thing I would start with is so many of these taxes were implicit taxes. That, of course, allows politicians to say they didn't change taxes, because they use the word narrowly to their advantage. So the political economists might explain that. More surprising, I think, is that the experts, not the politicians, offer opinions about the employment situation without mentioning these new taxes. I'm talking about the Federal Reserve or the IMF (International Monetary Fund). Now maybe the students of George Stigler and Gary Becker would say, "Come on, we can use political economy theory to explain . . . those are government institutions. We'll use political economy to explain why they don't do the economics quite right."

I think Gary would push back, but I think maybe economic education does have something to do with public policy. I'm going to side with the younger Milton Friedman, and I think all of us who learned from Gary need to do our part to pass on the economic way of thinking, because it doesn't pass itself on.

Question and Answer Session

QUESTION: *I would just offer what I'm sure Gary's spirit (which was quite influential in my early work on taxation, including taxation of the family and taxation of human capital) that he'd appreciate or might support a friendly amendment which would say: this doesn't yet get into all the negative effects on skill accumulation on people who are not in the labor force. And that would make things even worse.*

CASEY MULLIGAN: We need to go through these laws and ask, "What are they doing to the tax rate, not just on work but on human capital accumulation, on the job training, certain types of schooling?" It's really important. I haven't done it yet. It's doable, but I haven't done it. I'm hoping these effects take longer to accumulate, so I have time to catch up with the new laws. But of course, human capital is ultimately the number one thing to study in these sorts of situations.

QUESTION: *You've identified the behavioral effects and they look like they're potentially large. So the question is, what about the consequences for income distribution? Have you looked at disability, food stamps, ACA, individually or together, and their effects on income distribution?*

MULLIGAN: Although human capital definitely creates inequality in earnings, I think of it as fairly constant over this time frame. As I showed in my cross-sectional analysis, these aren't random samples of people who are leaving work. So redistribution is raising inequality. I think in a full analysis, though, you would want to look at those returns to human capital. That's a big deal for inequality issues. People who earn more probably have more human capital, and if we want to understand the distribution of earnings, you've got to understand the distribution of human capital. I haven't offered much on that, I'm afraid.

QUESTION: *You had mentioned when you showed your hours of work and you made the point that it's usually stated that during recessions, the less educated get hit more than the more educated. And you showed with hours of work, that wasn't the case. Now I'm thinking back to unemployment rates, and my sense is that with unemployment rates, that is the case, but that may not be right. Is it because I'm thinking of absolute changes versus proportionate changes? And you did proportionate changes? Or is there a difference between the intensive and the extensive margin?*

MULLIGAN: From the very beginning of this project, I never emphasized the unemployment rate. I'm sorry. I know what it means to be employed. Unemployed, I'm not sure what it means, number one. Number two, the payments to calling yourself unemployed versus out of the labor force are changing over this very period. My brain's not big enough to analyze that type of data, so I never looked at it.

QUESTION: *You mentioned, if I understood this distinction between single and married. The bottom line: is this a huge disincentive to marriage?*

MULLIGAN: I put it below human capital on the list of projects, but yes, the Affordable Care Act has big taxes on being married. And that's going to matter for families. And I think you want to quantify the size of those taxes and start to understand what to expect from families going forward under these new incentives. And the basic problem is that the subsidies are based on household income. And you're not a household if you're unmarried for tax purposes, but you are if you're married. So you can go from being below poverty to above poverty just by getting a marriage certificate. And that kicks a lot of people off these various forms of assistance. I'm sure people are going to consider that in their marriage behavior.

QUESTION: *I had a question about whether we are headed toward a European-style labor market because of this, where eligible jobs with large companies are very rare, and most other employment is temporary. And also, what do your findings say about whether the US will be a 2 percent growth economy or a 3.5 percent growth economy?*

MULLIGAN: To the first question, one puzzle a lot of guys here worked on—I know Gary worked on it; he and I talked about it together and this is a conversation the profession had in the eighties and nineties—why is the United States' public policy different from Europe's? There was a lot of head-scratching on that problem. But we don't have to scratch our heads anymore because we're going to be more like them. Our taxes are more hidden, more implicit. Theirs are more aboveboard. They have a payroll tax, a big one. And we have more hidden stuff. But other than that, the basic economics of redistribution are starting to look more and more similar all the time.

QUESTION: *If you go to Singapore, you learn they are allergic to stuff being thrown around and distributed. So one day, I went to the races on Sunday. And what do you do at the races? You bet, you lose, you tear up your ticket, and you throw it on the ground. Well, in Singapore, after each race, there's an announcement. In the upper right-hand corner of each ticket there is a number. And on Monday morning, there will be a drawing. The winning number gets a thousand dollars. They have no problem. So people respond to incentives. And it seems to me in listening to your presentation, even if things are implicit, people somehow sense them and they respond. So let me put my question this way, is there any result that you got in your work that was surprising?*

MULLIGAN: To the guys who took Gary's class, I don't think so. It's not cutting-edge stuff that I'm doing. I'm just measuring.

QUESTION: *So I know your work is focused on 2007 or more recently, but there's lots of changes in policy over longer periods, which people studied and I actually think it's pretty consistent with what you have. But that also shows that policy can change. You can see, partly because of the knowledge of the economics, it could be that the Chicago School itself waved back and forth. And your poll of the [University of] Chicago Booth School [of Business] would suggest it's waving in another direction. So based on the longer history, could you add more to your findings about whether we might find something to be more optimistic about going down the road? Or are we sort of continuing in this mode for a while? You can sort of see changes from the seventies to eighties, for example. People documented that. But could you comment a little bit on that?*

MULLIGAN: I'm kind of stuck on that. Friedman thought the ideas were important, and Stigler thought there were more basic forces there. Both things will change. Basic forces don't stay constant, and ideas don't stay constant.

QUESTION: *Casey, I'm curious. I'm right with you, and I think most people in this room are, on the negative effects of unemployment insurance and the extension up to ninety-nine weeks. I think there was even some research by President Obama's chief economist that affirmed unemployment insurance causes an uptick in the unemployment rate. So it made that dissonance really interesting. Can you give us an update on what the status is of the program now? I know it phased out. And what you thought about good ideas for replacing or reforming the unemployment insurance system.*

MULLIGAN: I showed a number of programs related to unemployment. The ninety-nine weeks has expired. The COBRA assistance has expired. The food stamp expansions are not expired, may never be expired. But the Affordable Care Act is that COBRA program all over again but for a bigger population. You don't have to be unemployed anymore. To get COBRA assistance, you had to say, "I'm looking for work." To get Obamacare, you don't need to say, "I'm looking for work." Just don't be at a job where they offer coverage. So you could be early retired. You could be a housewife, a house-husband. Not working is a source of assistance there, and it's a lot of assistance that's being directed. So you had some unemployment programs replacing others. I don't think you've had a reduction in assistance for non-employment.

FOLLOW-UP: *I know your focus has been on the health care law. It's been amazing. But just thinking—even if we're just with twenty-six weeks at roughly 50 percent replacement rate, aren't there better ways to help people to create maybe automatic stabilizers, some of the benefits to restructure when the program starts? Just for example, right now you lose your job, and you're immediately eligible for UI, that very first week. And this is one of the frustrating things when I came out of the military, that you could file for unemployment insurance right away. And then we wonder why there's a veteran's unemployment problem. Maybe if you had to wait for a month or two, but you had a more generous compensation, would that be a good idea? I'm just wondering on that program, if you've done any thinking or if you could point to some other scholars who've done some good research.*

MULLIGAN: Let me say the health reform that (Massachusetts Governor Mitt) Romney had, one of the big differences was RomneyCare had assistance for unemployed, but you had to wait six months to get that assistance. And with the ACA, there's no wait. That's a difference, so you could study that difference. I'm not saying which policy is better or worse, but you could study that one. You know, I came to Chicago very interested in optimal tax and optimal policy, and Gary talked me out of that quickly. He said, "Try to figure out what people do and worry about the optimal policy later." And I've followed that.

CHAPTER SIX

Income and Wealth in America

Kevin M. Murphy and Emmanuel Saez

In this session, Kevin Murphy and Emmanuel Saez present their research, react to each other's presentations, and take questions from the audience.

Part I: Kevin Murphy

I'm going to go relatively quickly because I think the discussions are always the best part. We've talked a lot about the top 1 percent. I'm not going to talk about the top 1 percent. I'm going to talk about the other 99 percent almost entirely. Before I start with the facts, I want to make sure that we're all thinking about it the same way. The most important thing, when we talk about wages and talk about inequality, is to realize that we're talking about prices. At least when you talk about wages, it's the price of labor that's being determined in some marketplace out there. I think that we sometimes tend to forget that. Prices matter. For example, what happens when you see the price of something go up? Why did it happen? Maybe demand went up or supply went down. How is the market going to respond?

If there's more demand for something than there was last year, people are going to produce more of it. These are the natural kinds of supply-and-demand responses that we expect to see in the marketplace. That's the perspective that I think is very important when thinking about the labor market. One thing at which I

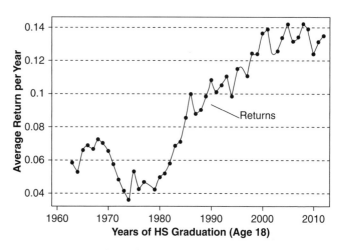

FIGURE 6.1. Returns to college education, 1963–2012
Source: Based on previous work done by Katz and Murphy (1992) updated to 2012

looked was returns to college. We've heard a lot about education and about returns to college. Figure 6.1 is a measure of returns to college in the United States.

The key feature on which you might focus is that there was a decline in the returns to college in the 1970s, which was actually a period where people were talking about Americans being over-educated. That was followed by the dramatic rise that occurred during the 1980s, a continued rise in the 1990s, and a relatively flat premium in the 2000s. What I hadn't really fully appreciated until the discussion over the last few days is that the timing of 1980 to 2000 as the big transition period is true for things beyond the college premium and wage inequality. A lot of the graphs that we saw the other day and a lot of the discussions that we heard yesterday on inequality at the top of the income distribution mirrored that same picture. A lot of what happened at the top of the income distribution happened pre-2000. That's certainly the case here when we look at the returns to college.

The other thing to note is just how dramatic that change is. The early-human-capital literature of the 1960s talked about the 7 percent return. It actually fell to maybe 5 percent in the 1970s. That was the "overeducated America" period. Now, you get returns more like 13 percent. It's really quite dramatic. Again, think about it in terms of prices. If you think about college as an investment, this would suggest that there's an enormous return to investment today—roughly triple what is was in 1980. At the same time, think about this as a price from the point of view of driving inequality in terms of the outcomes. It's like when the price of oil goes up. All of the guys who have oil are much better off than they were before, and all of the people who need to buy gas are worse off than they were before. That's part of the story. The other side is that there's a big incentive now to go out and to find more oil and to produce more oil than you did in the past. That's going to be true in the college market as well.

Figure 6.2 gives the change in the log wage rate over a roughly forty-year period from 1970–72 to 2010–12 for men and women by percentile of the wage distribution. These are different people at the beginning and end, and I'm matching the median in 1970 with the median in 2010. What we are asking is: how did the wages associated with different points in that distribution change over time? There are several interesting things about a figure like this, which will be part of the story when thinking about inequality.

One is to remember the timing. It's going up. It's not all the last ten years. It's been going up over time, but the other is that this is an upward-sloping line throughout the range. There's a bigger increase at the eightieth percentile than there was at the sixtieth and more at the sixtieth than at the fortieth. There's been growth in inequality throughout the distribution. This is not unique to the top. In fact, if you ask, how big is the gap between the middle and the top, the middle in the graph is about 0.2, and the top is almost

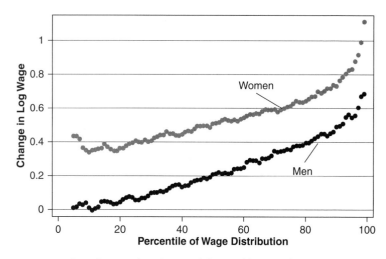

FIGURE 6.2. Growth in men's and women's log weekly wages by percentiles of the wage distribution, 1970–72 through 2010–12

Source: Based on previous work done by Katz and Murphy (1992) updated to 2010–2012

0.5. If you asked, how would I extrapolate out to the kinds of numbers you'd get way up there, maybe you get 0.7, which would be roughly a doubling of relative wages.

What's interesting is that this phenomenon, which is present throughout the distribution, parallels what has happened at the very top of the distribution. One really important question that needs to be answered is: is this the same phenomenon? Is it a related phenomenon? Are these two independent things that have happened? The last one is very unlikely. The question is: to what extent are they cousins, versus siblings? That's a really interesting question. I'm going to talk about some of the same explanations, although I'm not sure that the mechanisms are exactly the same for explaining what happened in the top. However, I believe they are closely related.

The other thing that you should not lose in this graph, and it was brought up earlier today, is that there's a major dimension in which inequality has fallen, and that is between women and men.

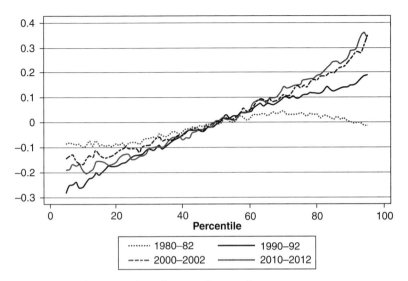

FIGURE 6.3. Change in relative log wage for men from 1970–82

Source: Based on previous work done by Katz and Murphy (1992) updated to 2010–2012

Women's wages were below men's. In this *graph* you can see that no matter whether you're talking with low-wage women or high-wage women, women have done much better than men over this forty-year period to the tune of almost twenty log points. That's a big change in relative wages.

Now, Figure 6.3 is the picture by time. Growth over the forty years is broken out by decade. For all of the curves, growth is measured from 1970–72 to the indicated period. The dotted line is what happened between 1970 and 1980–1982, those first ten years. The contrast between the people who gained the most and those who gained the least was mostly in the lower half. Inequality grew in the 1970s, but mostly in the lower half of the distribution. The 1990s have a large change. Inequality went up a lot at the top; it continued to fall at the bottom. There was growth in inequality both at the top and at the bottom. When you get to the 1990s, at the top, you continue to see rising inequality. On the bottom, we're moving slightly the other way. That's this kind of hollowing in the middle about which people often talk for that 1990s period. Then, you go to the 2000s. We see a modest increase at the top and a modest fall backward more like the 1980s at the bottom. The recent years are like a muted version of the 1980s with growth at both the top and the bottom.

Why has inequality increased? Here is what I think has been going on: the growth in inequality can be understood in terms of some of the most basic economic forces—supply and demand. I was a student of Gary Becker, so I don't know anything else. The demand for education and for other skills has been growing. I want to emphasize other skills—skills other than education. There's a tendency, when people think about human capital, to think about human capital as synonymous with education. Education explains a small amount of the variation in individual earnings. The r-squared in a regression, if you just put education in there, is around 0.1 to 0.2. It's a really low number. It doesn't explain a whole lot. There are lots of other skills out there. We focus on education because we can measure it, not because it is more important than other skills. A lot of other things are going on as well. There are a lot of other skills that are important.

In the basic model of supply and demand, when supply grows faster than demand, prices fall. When demand grows faster than supply, prices rise. The story actually turns out to fit the data very well. Figure 6.4 is a model that Larry Katz and I first estimated. I don't have an updated version of this, unfortunately. Larry Katz and I developed this model back in 1987 with data through 1987, so it's way before the end of the data in the graph. Basically, we were trying to explain why the college premium first fell in the 1970s and rose in the 1980s. The basic idea was that the 1970s were different because supply grew so fast. The big reason that supply grew so fast actually was the Baby Boom. There was a huge influx of educated young workers who flooded the market, pushing down

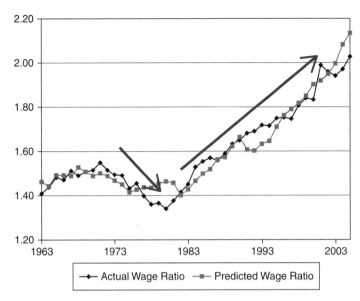

FIGURE 6.4. Supply growth and relative wages

Source: Based on previous work done by Katz and Murphy (1992) updated to 2005

prices. And then when supply growth slowed and demand didn't keep up, prices started going up.

This view of the world is important because the forces that generate growth in the demand for skilled labor are the same basic forces that generate economic progress. Think of it this way: where does progress come from? We have new technologies. We invest in physical capital to support those new technologies. Both technology and capital tend to be complements for skilled labor and substitutes for unskilled labor. We have a perpetual rise in the relative demand for skilled labor relative to unskilled labor. That's not new. That didn't start in 1980. That's been going on decade after decade throughout the twentieth century. Over the twentieth century, we increased the supply of skilled labor. If you look at education, we increased average education levels almost a year per decade over that period of time. As long as supply growth was keeping pace with the demand growth, returns to skill would not change in spite of growing demand. What's happened is that that relationship has broken down. Supply is no longer keeping pace with the ongoing growth in demand.

Now that's a bit too simplified, because if you look at the pattern of the change in the growth of demand, it has become more concentrated. You get that concave shape in the early years and more convex shape in the later years. There are subtleties to the story. I think that the data fit those nuances very well, but I will leave that aside for now. The key point is that this supply-and-demand view of the world is important.

What are the lessons that come out of this? One is that supply matters. That is, if you have low-skilled individuals earning low wages, if you can educate some of those people, improve their schooling, move them up the ladder, that will benefit them, and it will benefit all of the other low-skilled people by reducing the

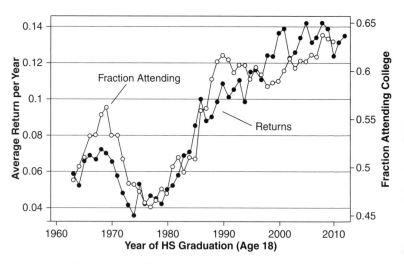

FIGURE 6.5. Returns and college attendance

Source: Based on previous work done by Katz and Murphy (1992) updated to 2012

supply of low-skilled competitors in the labor market, raising wages for the rest of the low-skilled population. Supply matters. You might ask, why has supply not kept pace? Do people not see the rise in demand and respond to it? Has supply responded? Figure 6.5 shows the returns to college and the fraction of high-school graduates who go to college. I'd say they responded. It looks pretty interesting actually. That is the return on one axis and the fraction attending on the other.

What's really interesting to me—and this gets to a point that George Shultz made yesterday—I was one of the early people to write on the college premium. Yet people started responding years before we started writing. I don't know what they were reading, or what data set they were looking at, but they obviously got the data before we did. What's interesting is that if you look at how many people graduate, not at how many people attend, it lags far behind. There are a lot of people who are starting college but, particularly among men, the number actually graduating doesn't respond nearly as much. To me, that suggests something very simple: there are a lot of people who see the need to go to college, who see the need to get more human capital more generally, but who are not well-prepared to do it.

That gets back to an important point about human capital: a key input into producing human capital is human capital itself. Human capital is human-capital-intensive. It takes the human capital of schoolteachers. It takes the human capital of parents. It takes your own human capital to help you succeed in school. You can't go to college if you had a lousy elementary and secondary education. When you have a poor elementary and secondary education, it is very difficult to be successful in college. The fact that more people are trying to go to college but are not being successful suggests that we have a big problem with preparation. A number of people are poorly prepared to go to school. That is not new. We've always had lots of people who are poorly prepared to go to college, poorly prepared to acquire human capital. The difference is that, in the past, there were lots of things for them to do. Now there are not as many things for low-skilled workers to do, since technology has progressed. Do we want to stop progress? No. The answer is that we've got to respond.

Go back to figure 6.1, which showed the returns to college. There are two ways to look at this. One is that supply has fallen short. The other is that there is an opportunity here. The best way to solve this shortage is to take advantage of the high return that the shortage has generated. That is, we've got an opportunity to get a return on investment that's higher than it's been in the past. That's assuming that we can actually invest in the skills that are reflected in these higher prices. I don't see any reason why we can't.

The second is that because the number of people going on to college (the extensive margin) has not kept pace with demand, prices have risen.

That generates an intensive margin response that exacerbates inequality because what happens is that the high-skilled people are supplying more labor. They're working harder. They're working more hours. They're investing more in themselves. They're moving to places that demand more human capital. This, unlike growth in the number of individuals completing college, actually increases inequality. Bob Topel and I have a paper that shows why that's the case. You've got technology working to increase inequality. The extensive margin is constantly pushing that back. When the extensive margin falls short, the intensive margin pushes inequality up because people are responding positively to their earnings. They're realizing that they can earn more. They're going to work harder, to work more, and to do things that bring more compensation.

Part II: Emmanuel Saez

I am going to talk about income and wealth and equality in America. I'm going to lay out the facts relatively quickly because we've seen, over these two days, a lot of those numbers already. And then I'll throw in some policy ideas to stimulate the debate. I've worked on top-income shares. Let me first say, this is a conference on inequality. Inequality matters because the public cares about it. That is, people evaluate their own success relative to others. People have a sense of fairness. That's why the study of inequality is interesting, and that's why we need economics to provide measures that are understandable to the public to illuminate the debate. We need to find simple ways to measure inequality, so what we've done is that we've measured shares of total income going to the top 10 percent, top 1 percent, etc. We've used individual income tax statistics because they are the only source that cover long time periods and that capture top incomes well. Thomas Piketty started this literature with the study of France, and I analyzed with him the case of the United States.

I'm going to talk about pre-tax market income. That is what people earn on the market before taxes and before transfers from the government. As a caveat, I want to point out that the numbers you'll see, and that you've seen yesterday, are narrower than national income. They include market income reported on tax returns and, hence, they exclude things like employer-provided health care benefits or imputed rent of homeowners. Our next goal is to broaden the series to reflect total income, so that we will be able to distribute national income on a pre-tax, pre-transfer basis and also do it on a post-tax, post-transfer basis.

Figures 6.6 and 6.7 show the facts for the United States. If you look at the share of income going to the top 10 percent families, it has that big U shape over the last hundred years. There was a very high level of income concentration before World War II, with the top 10 percent getting 45 percent of total income. There was a big fall in income concentration during World War II, and then a period of much lower income concentration in the following three decades. What is striking indeed has been the surge in the

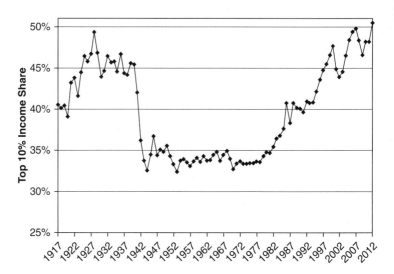

FIGURE 6.6. Top 10 percent pre-tax income share in the US, 1917–2012

Source: Thomas Piketty and Emmanuel Saez, "Income Inequality in the United States, 1913–1998," *Quarterly Journal of Economics* 118 (1) (2003), updated to 2012

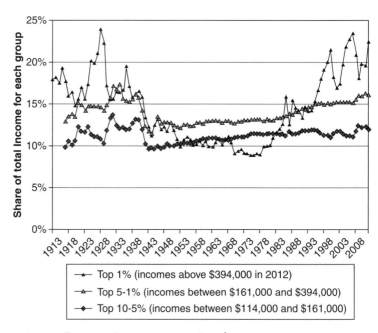

FIGURE 6.7. Decomposing top 10 percent into three groups, 1913–2012

Source: Thomas Piketty and Emmanuel Saez, "Income Inequality in the United States, 1913–1998," *Quarterly Journal of Economics* 118 (1) (2003), updated to 2012

last three or four decades where the top 10 percent income share goes from 33 percent all the way to 50 percent, so that in recent years we are at a level of income concentration that is as high as it's been over the last hundred years. The second fact that echoes what Kevin Murphy was showing is that this effect has been really very highly concentrated. The higher you go in the distribution, the bigger the gain. Figure 6.7 displays the top 1 percent, next 4 percent (top 5-1%), and next 5 percent (top 10-5%) income shares. You can see that out of the seventeen-point increase in the top 10 percent income share, most of that comes from the top 1 percent, whose income share goes from slightly below 10 percent to above 20 percent in recent years with some gains in the next 4 percent and with only a little bit of gain in the next 5 percent.

What is driving top-income shares? If you look at the worldwide evidence that we've gathered, all currently rich countries had very high levels of income concentration a hundred years ago. That's true for Sweden. Even the most equal countries today had very high levels of income concentration a century ago. Income concentration fell dramatically in all countries in the first half of the twentieth century. Income concentration surged back in some—but not in all—countries since the 1970s. Chad Jones showed numbers. In the US, you've seen that income concentration has increased dramatically. In France, as well as in other continental European countries and in Japan, the increase has been much smaller, which tells you that globalization cannot be the sole explanation (see Atkinson, Piketty, and Saez 2011 for international evidence on top income shares). What matters is how globalization interacts with institutions or with the market structure in each country.

One of the things we've looked at is the role of progressive taxation. What we've found is that the surge in pretax top incomes is highly correlated with measures of tax progressivity measured in a very simple way by the top marginal income tax rate. So, figure 6.8 is the cross-country evidence from the 1960s to the recent period.

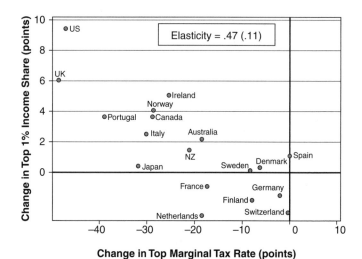

FIGURE 6.8. Change in top tax rate and top 1 percent share, 1960–4 to 2005–9

Source: Thomas Piketty, Emmanuel Saez, and Stefanie Stantcheva, "Optimal Taxation of Top Labor Incomes: A Tale of Three Elasticities," *American Economic Journal: Economic Policy* 6 (1) (2014)

On the x-axis, we put the cut in the top marginal tax rate over that period, and so you have two outliers, the United States and the United Kingdom. They were the countries that had the highest top marginal tax rates back in the 1960s, and they are the ones who cut them the most. And then on the y-axis, you have the change in the top 1 percent pretax-income shares. Here it's pretax, so that there's no mechanical relationship between tax rates and top incomes. You see that countries are aligned roughly on the diagonal; the countries that cut their top tax rates the most experienced the biggest increase in top income shares. A number of countries in Europe who didn't change their tax policy, and they didn't experience a very large change in income concentration.

Figure 6.9 shows the striking inverse relationship in the United States between the top 1 percent pretax income share that we've

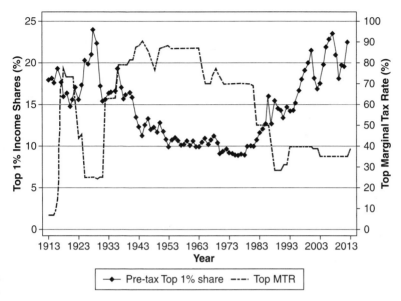

FIGURE 6.9. Top 1 percent income share (pre-tax) and top marginal tax rate

Source: Thomas Piketty, Emmanuel Saez, and Stefanie Stantcheva, "Optimal Taxation of Top Labor Incomes: A Tale of Three Elasticities," *American Economic Journal: Economic Policy* 6 (1) (2014)

seen and, in the dotted line on the right-hand-side y-axis, the top marginal income tax rate that has an inverse U-shape over the century with very high top tax rates in excess of 70 percent from 1933 to 1981. The two curves mirror each other. How do we interpret these strong links between top income shares and top tax rates? One view, natural to economists, is that it reflects a supply-side response. That is, in the recent period, high earners didn't have to pay as much in marginal taxes, so they worked more, they generated more economic activity, and they earned more. Another view that Josh Rauh discussed in his presentation is that they worked more, but not in a productive way, but rather they worked more at extracting more pay. Think about academics like myself. If tax rates are low, I'm going to chase offers from high-paying places to increase my salary but I am not necessarily going to work more on my research. I have more incentives to get a big pay increase if the tax rates are low because I can keep a larger fraction of my pay increases.

It's very hard to distinguish between those two stories. I'm not going to nail it today, but I think that this is a critical question to understand regarding what we should do about tax policy and top earners. Figure 6.10 shows striking evidence on the pattern of real growth per adult in the United States for the bottom 99 percent and top 1 percent starting from a base of one hundred in 1913 and going all the way to 2012. In the long run, economic growth lifts all boats so that the top 1 percent and the bottom 99 percent average incomes have been multiplied by roughly a factor of four over a century from 1913 to 2012. However, what is striking here is how different the timing of growth is for the top 1 percent vs. the bottom 99 percent.

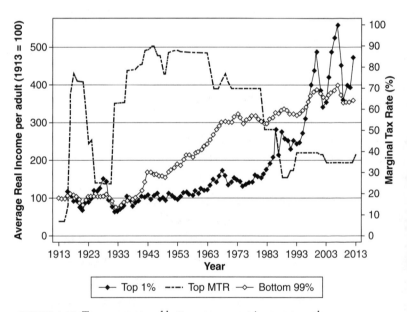

FIGURE 6.10. Top 1 percent and bottom 99 percent income growth

Source: Thomas Piketty, Emmanuel Saez, and Stefanie Stantcheva, "Optimal Taxation of Top Labor Incomes: A Tale of Three Elasticities," *American Economic Journal: Economic Policy* 6 (1) (2014)

That is, if you look at the period when top tax rates were very high, you had strong growth for the bottom 99 percent and low growth for the top 1 percent. The pattern switched starting in the 1970s in the period where top tax rates went down dramatically. You had a very large increase in top 1 percent incomes and a slowing down of the bottom 99 percent income growth. This is a striking graph because it shows you that over a period of a few decades the growth experienced for different groups can be very different. People have talked a lot about the recent period. The Great Recession hit the top 1 percent and the bottom 99 percent. Coming out of the Great Recession, we see very little growth for the bottom 99 percent and a quick recovery for the top 1 percent.

Now, let me talk briefly about what we can say about wealth inequality. Income and savings create wealth. I've done a study recently with Gabriel Zucman using capital income-tax data to capitalize income and to get a long-time series of wealth inequality. If you look at the bottom 90 percent wealth share in the United States, you do see a significant increase with the democratization of wealth ownership of, first, housing, then of pensions. But starting in the mid-1980s, you see an erosion of middle-class wealth, where their share goes from a peak of 36 percent down to the low 20s. And so for the top 1 percent wealth share, you get the inverse, with a big U, and a significant increase again, going from the low 20s percent in the late 1970s to 42 percent in recent years. It looks like wealth inequality evolves similarly to income inequality. Figure 6.12 shows absolute real wealth per family from 1946 to 2012. On the right y-axis, you have in dollars the wealth of the bottom 90 percent, and on the x-axis, multiplied by one hundred, is top 1 percent wealth. Both measures increase; but, again, the Great Recession dramatically hit the bottom 90 percent, with no recovery afterward. Today, the bottom 90 percent finds itself with a wealth level similar to the 1980s. In contrast, the top 1 percent was hit a little bit, but then the upward trend resumed quickly.

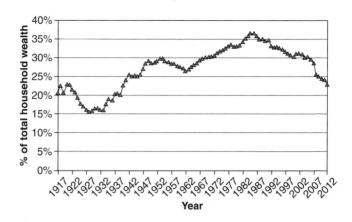

FIGURE 6.11. Bottom 90 percent wealth share in the United States, 1917–2012

Source: Emmanuel Saez and Gabriel Zucman, "Wealth Inequality in the United States since 1913: Evidence from Capitalized Income Tax Data," National Bureau of Economic Research, Working Paper No. 20625, 2014

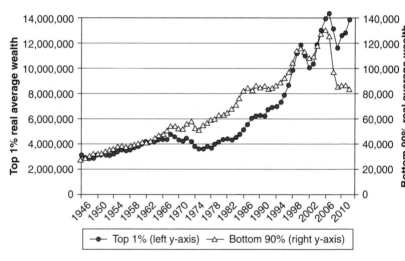

FIGURE 6.12. Real average wealth of bottom 90 percent and top 1 percent families

Source: Emmanuel Saez and Gabriel Zucman, "Wealth Inequality in the United States since 1913: Evidence from Capitalized Income Tax Data," National Bureau of Economic Research, Working Paper No. 20625, 2014

By combining income and wealth, we can figure out what are the savings rates that are consistent with the patterns that we find. The erosion of wealth of the bottom 90 percent is related to the savings rate. It's true that incomes didn't do too well, but the relative decline in wealth is so large that even if you take into account price effects, it has to be explained by a very low savings rate for the bottom 90 percent. We find ourselves in a world in which income inequality is increasing, the bottom 90 percent families save less, and, therefore, their wealth doesn't make progress. And now, if you look at savings rate by wealth class, the top 1 percent had very high savings rates. At least that's what you need to explain how their wealth has increased so much, even taking into account that their incomes have increased.

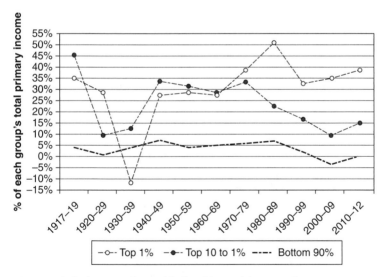

FIGURE 6.13. Savings rates by wealth class (decennial averages)

Source: Emmanuel Saez and Gabriel Zucman, "Wealth Inequality in the United States since 1913: Evidence from Capitalized Income Tax Data," National Bureau of Economic Research, Working Paper No. 20625, 2014

The last fact that I want to point out relates to what Josh Rauh presented yesterday. It looks like the top wealth holders have significantly more income and, in particular, labor income. They are also younger if you look at the data. It looks like the surge in top incomes combined with high savings rates has led to the creation of new fortunes. We find ourselves in a world where there is much more correlation between labor income and wealth. Based on that, what should we think about policy? If you want to prevent ever-growing wealth and income concentration, what should you be doing? The estate tax is the most direct tool to prevent self-made wealth from becoming inherited wealth. That is, if we see this huge increase in wealth concentration, and if we look at charitable-giving data, and we don't see the rich giving away a growing fraction of their income, if that hasn't changed that much over time, it has to be the case that the flow of inheritance at the top is going to increase.

Another element based on Gary Becker's work is the human capital transmission channel. I believe it is becoming very important because richer families can devote more resources to children's education. High-wealth, high-income people are going to put the effort to make sure that they navigate the school system and get the best possible education for their kids. Statistics on parental income of students in top universities are really striking (see Chetty et al. 2015). In top universities, think about the Harvards and the Stanfords, over 50 percent of students come from top 10 percent families. Over 20 percent of students come from top 1 percent families; the human capital channel is going to be very important. We need to find ways to promote access to top schools for low-income talented kids. Caroline Hoxby and Chris Avery have fascinating work showing that a large fraction of talented but low-income kids don't seem to be able to optimize the system. They would be admitted to the Stanfords and to the Harvards with very low tuition because of financial aid, and yet they don't apply to such schools. They just don't know how to navigate the process.

Rebuilding middle-class incomes is possibly the hardest problem to solve. There are limits to increasing direct means-tested transfers. First, there is the issue of marginal tax rates that Casey Mulligan pointed out at the beginning of the conference. More redistribution through means-tested transfers means higher marginal tax rates; and for the low-income families, high tax rates on earnings matter in terms of their work decision. Second, I don't think that the US public is in favor of increased direct support for redistribution from the government. What the public really wants is for the market economy to deliver a more equal distribution of income pretax. Kevin Murphy has talked a lot about schools, and I agree with him. We can discuss that more now. Think about policies that can reshape the distribution of pretax income. I talked about progressive taxes at the top. Minimum wages at the bottom, union policies, also seem quite a bit correlated with pretax income inequality.

In terms of rebuilding middle-class wealth, we have seen that bottom 90 percent wealth is stagnating, mostly due to plummeting savings rates. And now, why have savings rates fallen so much? It could be stagnating incomes coupled with a desire to keep up your consumption. That combined with financial deregulation, offering ways for people to borrow, with the subprime mortgages being the most striking example. All of that of course requires some present-biased consumption behavior from individuals. So, how do we think about encouraging savings of the bottom 90 percent families? I think that here we have very good work coming out of behavioral economics showing that default choices have much more impact than tax incentives for savings. The best examples come from the 401(k) literature. When employers make you pay into the 401(k) with contributions, by default, we do see an enormous impact on overall contributions.

Chetty et al. (2014) have done very good work in Denmark, showing that there were higher pension contributions when that was made the default decision. Such defaults actually translate into more wealth accumulation because individuals don't offset that with reduced savings in other accounts. In the United States, there is a debate about expanding nudged savings through automatic IRAs, so that this type of default savings tool is available to people who do not have access to 401(k)s (Thaler and Sunstein 2008). The fact that we observe opt-out defaults in private 401(k) plans suggests that there is indeed a need here that the market is trying to fill, but that might not reach the bottom 50 percent individuals who work in jobs that don't offer 401(k)s. That's a place where we can think about light government interventions to rebuild middle-class wealth.

Moderator: Let me give you each a chance to comment briefly on what each other has said. Listening to you, it seems to me there are kind of two different views of why this has happened. Kevin has emphasized education quite a bit. And I think that Emmanuel has focused on marginal tax rates more. Certainly there's a difference there that's quite clear. And, of course, there are different solutions, but that does lead you in two different directions.

Murphy: I'll go back to saying just how broad-based the growth and inequality are. It's hard to believe that top marginal tax rates are really the drivers of that. One of the things that suggest a human capital explanation is that if you look at hours by percentiles of the distribution, you see a big steepening of the hours profile, where the higher-wage people are working a lot harder and lower-wage people are working less. Even theory doesn't say that I would see a response mostly in the form of rent-seeking. There is a greater return to getting more income. For lots of people there isn't a great opportunity, I don't think, for rent-seeking, but there is a positive-feedback effect. I think that that is an important feature. The situation has opened up opportunities and rewards for people with high levels of human capital. People earn more on lots of margins.

It's not just hours. When we talk about labor supply, we always think about hours, but a lot of it is effort, and a lot of it is occupational choice. There are lots of other dimensions. I think that a key question is: how closely tied are those things going on at the very top with the things going on in the middle and top? They're very coincidental time-wise.

The second thing that is really important is this question of human capital. I think that we're probably in agreement that human capital is incredibly important. I would encourage people to work on the human-capital area because it's very different than physical capital. You go to work and you work with a sophisticated piece of equipment, you go home at night, and it stays at work, and you go home. But the human capital you take home with you. It affects lots of outcomes, like your children and your health. We've seen a widening of health inequality among people by education level—partly, I think, for that same reason that human capital is a really important ingredient.

One thing that comes up on wealth is that part of the difference is that rich people and lower-income people have different kinds of wealth, so the composition of wealth can explain some of that. The other thing about which we don't talk there is of course human wealth. And for poor people human wealth is most of the wealth that they have by an overwhelming amount. And so you have to leverage the picture of the world when you look at their assets. The asset is a very small part of their overall budget constraint, so it's not surprising that they might go negative even on that one piece of the budget constraint in terms of their behavior.

Many people talk about market failures. I think that if you focused on markets, you'd get more discussion of how market improvements might lead to some things which we might not like. Think about credit constraints. If you have a credit constraint, it doesn't only apply to investing in your kids, it applies to all the things that you would do if you could get resources today. It's not surprising. If credit markets get better, guess what people who are credit-constrained will want to do? Not save. There was never a saving constraint. It was a borrowing constraint. They're going to borrow more than they would have otherwise. Now, you might not like the consequences of markets getting better. I think that markets have gotten better on so many margins that would generate the kinds of changes that we've seen. It doesn't mean that we want to make markets worse again. It just means that some of the issues that we have are going to show up in different ways.

Saez: I want to come back to the issue of human capital about which Kevin talked. If you look historically at what has been driving college attendance rates, the role of the government seems overwhelming here. That is, if you look at college graduation rates, you see a huge increase after World War II because of the GI Bill for men that you don't see for women. Here in California the master plan that was decided by former Governor Brown played a huge role in expanding access to higher education. When we see the retreat of state funding for higher education, the market substitutes that we get are the for-profit colleges that don't seem to be working nearly as well or as effectively as community colleges. That's why it's very hard for me to believe that education is like another good. My question is: could education ever be a good where people see the quality and know what they are shopping for? I'm not an expert, but of all the facts that I've seen, it strikes me that there are very big differences. People are not able to shop optimally for education.

The recent work by Hoxby and Avery (2013) was mind-boggling to me. You have in the United States many talented kids who could get into Stanford and Harvard, paying very little tuition, and yet they don't apply. That's why I'm not as confident as Kevin that a free market for education would improve education.

Murphy: I would say that the striking thing to me is not so much at higher education. I agree, to navigate that market requires some

education. I don't think that people from less-educated backgrounds, with parents from less-educated backgrounds, navigate
that market as well. But at least they have the opportunity to navigate that market. When it comes to elementary and secondary
education, so many people just don't even have the opportunity to
shop. They can shop in a variety of stores. They maybe don't want
to shop, and it may be hard to get to my neighborhood, and shop
in the stores in my neighborhood, but they can go there. In education, other people can't shop in my stores. I've got stores available
to me. There's a high school right next to my house to which lots of
people from the city of Chicago would love to go. They do not have
the opportunity to shop in that store.

Maybe there's 20 percent to 30 percent of those people who
wouldn't know that that's the store to go to, but there's 70 percent
or 80 percent of them who know quite well that they'd rather go
to that school than to the one that they're going to right now. In
fact, I would bet that 99 percent of them, if you asked them, do you
want to go to the one next to Kevin's house, or do you want to go to
your school, would say, "I want to go to the one by Kevin's house."
Today, it's not a market. There's a market for property, but then that
gets us into all of these other issues of how do you actually get into
that school. I think that the lack of a market in elementary and
secondary education is incredible.

We can try to tackle inequality on the back end, but that's an
inferior solution. Transferring people money, and thinking it is
going to make up for the lack of skills and education that those
people have, is not a good solution. In a world where you're doing
more and more health at home, you're doing less of it in the hospi-
tal. More and more, you're supposed to monitor your own health,
take your own drugs on time. Health, educating your kids, all of
this requires human capital. The tough part of this is that human
capital is an incredibly long-lived asset. It lasts a long time. Fixing
this problem is going to take a long time because we know that

you can't just go to all of the twelfth graders today and correct all of the mistakes you made in the first twelve years of education. That's a hard thing to do. If we fix it for kindergartners, it's going to be sixteen years before they graduate from college. It's going to be thirty-five years before they're half of the labor force. But, we've got to do it because it's important for their labor market success and their success in other areas like health. It's important for individuals but it is also important for other low-skilled people. To me, it's just got to be the way to go.

Saez: I totally agree that improving human capital is fundamental. I agree that in the current US system, public schools are too low-quality in too many places. The question is: how do we improve the schools? That's what we should be debating.

Murphy: But how do we do it? By spending more money? We already spend a lot of money. The Chicago schools are not cheap schools. They are not schools that lack for dollars. They've got lots of dollars flowing into them. They probably spend as much on that school to which no one wants to go as they spend on the school next to my house, maybe more. Now, maybe they need to spend even more than that, because we've got deficiencies in the household and things like that. But I'm skeptical as to whether pushing more money into that school is really going to be the answer. Forcing that school to compete for students, to me, is a much better thing to do.

Question and Answer Session

QUESTION: *The historical thing that I wanted to mention is that if you look at the early nineteenth century, when industrialization began to increase in England, it had a terrible effect on the lower-class peasants who were moving into cities. If you read John Hicks, for instance, you will see that it took a while for the rest of*

the population to benefit. The early industrialists benefited enor-
mously but, by the middle of the century, things began to improve
for a much larger group. Now, we live in a very similar period.
Two things have happened in the last ten years or twenty years.
One is globalization. The other one is the high-tech revolution.

Shouldn't we give it a bit of time? We're only looking at a ten-
year period, and you say that these wages have really gone up.
Well, that's because the rest of society hasn't caught up with it. To
acquire the kind of human capital about which Kevin Murphy
is talking, takes a while. It's not a magic wand that you can just
move, and then things will begin to catch up. We need to have
some time, so that the rest of society can also catch up with it.

SAEZ: Yes, it took a very long time for the technology progress
to translate into higher pretax income, but the second very big
transformation that you have is the increase in the size of government. In the nineteenth century, the government was taking in taxes around 10 percent of GDP in all countries. By the
mid-twentieth century, you're up to 35 percent for countries
like the United States and even higher in Europe. So, by developing the big programs about which we all know—education,
health insurance, and retirement—the government changed
things dramatically in terms of the distribution of income. In
terms of wealth, I agree with you that a lot of the reason that
middle-class wealth has eroded is taking on extra debt for college through student loans.

MURPHY: One thing that I would add on the college and savings
is that this gets the stuff about which Casey talked yesterday. It's
not just spending on college. There's an enormous tax on savings if you save to send your kids to college because of the way
that financial aid is calculated. They look at how much you can
afford to pay. They factor in about 40 percent of your savings.
It's incredible the tax rate that they put on savings and say, that's

how much we're going to reduce your access to either grants or loans, which clearly is going to have an effect above and beyond just actually spending. It doesn't pay to have it. The other one is the long history. One thing I think is important to think about is that we tend to think about steady-state models. I don't think the twentieth century, from the human capitalist perspective, looks like a steady state. We're spending more and more time, a bigger share of income, investing in human capital. The question is: was that going to keep going on forever? And was that going to inevitably lead to the supply side falling short of the demand side? I don't know, but it's something important to think about.

QUESTION: *Thank you both, of course, for interesting papers. I have a small question, though, about the data. And, I may be completely wrong, but I want to take us back to the 1980s when tax rates were very high. It almost became a national game to convert income into capital gains. People were doing all kinds of things to do that. There were then clubs formed. One dentist, one doctor, one lawyer, one carpenter, etc., who provided services. I wonder whether in fact part of what you see is actually not so much an increase in the incomes of the top as an increase in the recorded incomes once tax rates are lower, and therefore the amount of effort it takes to go into all of these activities is less profitable because you're not paying as much tax when you don't do it.*

SAEZ: Thank you very much for this question, which is very important, and indeed conservative commentators have looked at our numbers and said: "Look! This doesn't have anything to do with inequality. It might be just an artifact of tax avoidance. When tax rates are high, the rich are going to make sure to find ways to hide their income, so that it's not taxable." It is a very important question to address. Thomas Piketty and myself are also public economists so we are very interested in taxes and in behavioral response to taxation. We've looked for a lot of that. It is true that following tax episodes, you can see shifting of income from the corporate form to the individual form depending on which form of organization is tax-favored. So in the series that I have presented, indeed, we add back realized capital gains because a lot of the games for tax avoidance were through converting ordinary income into capital gains.

One simple piece of evidence that strongly suggests that the rich have indeed become richer comes from charitable giving, because charitable giving is tax-deductible. When tax rates are high, that's when you want to give to charities. Yet if you look at the pattern of charitable giving of those high-income people, the trend follows almost exactly parallel to their reported incomes. Top 1 percent income earners were giving around 4 percent of their reported income to charities in the 1960s. Today, they are giving about the same fraction of their reported income. Because top reported incomes have grown so fast, the charitable giving of the wealthy has also grown very fast. That shows you that their real incomes must have increased as well. Otherwise, how is it that they would be able to give so much more now when the tax incentive to give is smaller?

QUESTION: *I appreciate the necessity of looking at income and wealth data, but it seems like there's an invisible elephant in the room that should be paid attention to. That is, what is happening to consumption over time? I think a strong case can be made that, in many areas, the equality of consumption has increased. Ordinary people today, maybe in many cases poor Americans, can consume things that only the rich could consume just a generation or two ago. I think that it's an important fact. It's something that's often overlooked when we look at the monetary figures.*

MURPHY: I think that that's really important, and I've seen you present things on that. I've done things like that for my class where you really can see that a pair of jeans cost about the same at Wal-Mart as it did when I was a kid, to get a pair of jeans in nominal terms. Look at lots of other goods. I used to tell the story of the $5 iron that I bought. I bought an iron. I couldn't figure out how anybody in the world could make an iron, and put it in a box, and ship it to Target and sell it to me for $5. Those kinds of things are really amazing in terms of progress! You've got to take all of these price deflators with a grain of salt on the aggregate. The more interesting question is: should we be using differential deflators for different groups? I think there is some indication that that would undo some of the inequality that we see. However, I don't think that anybody's done enough to know exactly how to do that, but I think that it's an important question.

SAEZ: I agree. It is extremely important to look at consumption, but you see, with income, you pay taxes, and then you consume or you save. Savings go into wealth, so all of those things are linked. Our numbers suggest that the high incomes are saving a substantial fraction. In principle you could back out their consumption. Consumption inequality must have increased because I don't think that the surge in top incomes goes all into savings. Probably a significant chunk goes into consumption, but those are numbers we want to produce. I should say that, unfortunately, data on consumption and savings in the United States are really bad in part because we can only measure it through surveys. There's a lot of measurement error, and you cannot measure what happens for the top 1 percent with survey data. That's a problem if you want to evaluate serious proposals to shift to a progressive consumption tax. What we argue is that we should collect more. It wouldn't take that much extra by the US Treasury for tax enforcement purposes to collect a few more numbers about balances that would cast a lot of light on those issues of what is consumption inequality.

QUESTION: *Thank you. I just want to add a response to Kevin's response. If you look at, say, the price of Facebook. We know what it all is. It's zero. And so, when it's introduced, and it's introduced at a zero price, everyone gets that. It doesn't show up in anything. It doesn't show up in any consumption data, and yet it's enormously valuable for many people. The other thing I'm going to point out is if you look at the marginal tax-rate cut, it went from 70 percent down to 50 percent in 1982, went to 28 percent in 1987 or 1988. And so here's one source of income you really can't look at, interest on municipal bonds. You had high marginal tax-rate people in the 1970s buying municipal bonds like crazy because they could get a low rate, but it wasn't taxed at all at the federal level. Rate cuts happened. Through the 1980s, people shifted out of municipal bonds into taxable bonds. It then shows up as income on their tax form, and it didn't even show up as income on their tax form before. I grant your point about charity being one of the pieces of evidence to make me wonder on the margin. I just don't think that that's strong enough evidence to go against these things.*

SAEZ: Regarding municipal bonds, that's a good one to ask because for the wealth data, we have to distribute municipal bonds, so you see tax-exempt interest income from municipal bonds after 1986. What you find there is that the top 1 percent in 1987–1988, when we started seeing the data, already had something like 75 percent of all municipal bonds. So, we assume the top 1 percent wealthiest had 75 percent of all municipal bonds before 1986. At the maximum, they are going to have 100 percent of municipal bonds. So even if you make the extreme assumption that the top 1 percent held all of the municipal bonds, it's not going to have a large impact on the series, but that goes with the line of tax avoidance, etc. We, who study taxes and the behavioral responses they create, love that stuff, and we've been doing studies over the years, and we'll continue doing that. Your point is well-taken.

COMMENT: *We know that what is upsetting the public is not the fact that rich people are getting richer, it's the fact that middle-class people have taken a very substantial hit in income over the past six years. There's only one reason for that, and that's the crisis. If you look at wage rates, they have stayed on their trends. You don't see any. There's no evidence whatsoever of the effect of this crisis. It's all on the amount of work being done, and not on the amount that works gets per hour. I've done a lot of work recently on trying to understand why those effects should be so large and so durable. The output currently is about 13 percent below where it would have been without the crisis.*

That of course reflects directly into incomes. Part of it is the loss of the capital stock that occurred. That's quite big. It's over three percentage points of that. But the other big chunk is that participation in the labor force has declined. That coincides with an expansion of very badly designed benefit programs. This is obviously something on which Casey Mulligan is an expert, especially food stamps. The design of food stamps is a great puzzle to me, but there was a doubling in the food-stamp population, and most of that has remained. In fact, the food-stamp dependency has risen recently, in spite of the fact that the economy has been expanding, even though almost everyone says that the reason for that doubling was the rise in unemployment.

The decline in unemployment has not shown up in any significant diminution of food stamps. Food stamps have a 30 percent marginal tax rate, so not surprisingly, almost everyone on food stamps does not even consider participating. We need to take this seriously. The other big one of course is Social Security disability. A lot of very good work has been done about how that program should be changed to become a pro-work program as opposed to an anti-work program, which is what it is now. The same thing applies to food stamps. Food stamps have gotten much less attention even though the program has vastly more dependence.

QUESTION: *I have one comment, one quick technical question, and one broader question. Let me start with the technical question. Emmanuel, did you guys gross up your tax-dividend data to be consistent with the national accounts, because in addition to the changes in the tax laws, precisely over this period, there's been a series of changes in reporting requirements from financial institutions, for example, to report dividend payments. So, the question is, are you capturing that by trying to gross up to some non-tax-generated estimate of dividends by firms, for example?*

The second point is on price indexes. Our price indexes include the feeding in of consumer prices into the GDP deflator, which is a Fisher index, so that they don't have the substitution-bias issues, but it has a well-documented outlet substitution bias, precisely because the BLS (Bureau of Labor Statistics) keeps going back to the same outlets and assumes that people don't change where they shop or how they shop or even when they shop. They still collect data the second week of the month. So the fact that people buy stuff the week after Christmas or take advantage of sales doesn't get included.

My broader question is a generalization of an earlier point, a point that other people have made about what we're examining here. There's been an enormous increase in what some people have called Social Security or Medicare transfer wealth—that is, for the bottom part of the distribution. A large part of their wealth is annuitized real benefits that are going to be provided by the government. And so, I'm just wondering if you're going to look at that when you move to look at post-tax and transfer income. This also, because of those programs, is a period where we've transferred huge amounts of resources, actually and then prospectively even more from the young taxpayers to old consumers. That may be part of what's going on in the saving rate issue.

MURPHY: I agree on most of those issues. One thing that I would say is, when it comes to wealth on the housing side, it seems to me that you've always got to remember that it's on the other side of the budget constraint as well. So, when your wealth goes down because your house is worth less, particularly if you're a young person, it's not clear you really are worse off in a present-value sense because you needed a place to live for the rest of your life anyway. So, if I'm old and going to sell my house in ten years, that's a different story than if I'm a young guy. We always include the housing value, but we don't consider the cost, which is mirrored on the other side of the budget constraint.

SAEZ: Right now in our income measures we don't gross up to match national accounts, but as I said in my first slide, that's really the next point in our agenda. We have already put in place a lot of the elements to be able to distribute national income where everything will fit with the national accounts, and transfers will be taken into account no longer in the static way, perhaps in a dynamic way, perhaps along the lines you suggest.

QUESTION: *I want to take a step back and ask a more general question that pertains to Emmanuel Saez, and Chad Jones' talk yesterday, and even to Kevin Murphy. By far the biggest change over the past three decades is that a half billion people in the world went from extreme poverty to the middle class. That's a decline in income inequality. We keep talking about how world income inequality has gone up. That's because you do it within country rather than across the whole world. Now, that's important for a couple of reasons. First of all, it's important because it's not clear to me that the country is the relevant unit of analysis when I'm thinking of r – g.*

It may be that the world is the appropriate unit because we want to think about productivity for the world population growth and so forth. Emmanuel, I think, probably gave the best reason for why you'd want to do it within country, and that is that you have policies that are country-based. But even if I think about it in those terms, I think, "Well, what are the most important policies that have had to do with this major transformation in raising the incomes of the poor?"

We're talking about India and China, and I think there is simply no denying that the market reforms that occurred in the 1980s and 1990s in China and in the early 1990s in India are the single most important factor for raising the incomes of the poor. So I'm a heck of a lot more concerned about what's happened to the lowest 10 percent of the world than I am the upper 0.1 percent, and I'd like for you guys to comment on it. It's one part of the whole inequality debate that's been missed at this conference, and I think to my mind the most important part of it.

MURPHY: I agree that you want to take a worldwide perspective on these things. That is an important ingredient. It's related to what happens here. There is at least some spillover from those events to the events that we see in these countries. The reason that I think you still need to care about inequality is because I think that it will be a driver of policy. I think that you're going to do something. I think that Emmanuel is saying the same thing. It's going to push us to do something, and we'd better do something smart. If it pushes us to do something that improves the human capital side of things, that's actually a good thing.

SAEZ: I agree from a development perspective, the rise of incomes in low-income countries is the most important factor. Again, we share a lot of our incomes at the country level. Remember, governments in advanced economies take 35 percent to 50 percent of market incomes to fund public goods and the welfare state. Within a country, people are willing to share a substantial fraction of their income. You compare yourself not with people in China, but with people in your country. That's why the issue of inequality within country is for us to stay no matter what happens to economic growth.

References

Atkinson, Anthony, Thomas Piketty, and Emmanuel Saez. 2011. "Top Incomes in the Long Run of History." *Journal of Economic Literature* 49 (1): 3–71.

Chetty, Raj, John Friedman, Soren Leth-Petersen, Torben Nielsen, and Tore Olsen. 2014. "Active vs. Passive Decisions and Crowd-out in Retirement Savings Accounts: Evidence from Denmark." *Quarterly Journal of Economics* 129 (3): 1141–1219.

Chetty, Raj, John Friedman, Emmanuel Saez, Nicholas Turner, and Danny Yagan. 2015. "Does Higher Education Promote Opportunity or Maintain Privilege? Evidence from US Tax Data." *American Economic Review: Papers and Proceedings,* upcoming, May.

Hoxby, Caroline, and Christopher Avery. 2013. "The Missing 'One-Offs': The Hidden Supply of High-Achieving, Low-Income Students." *Brookings Papers on Economic Activity,* Spring: 1–65.

Piketty, Thomas, and Emmanuel Saez. 2003. "Income Inequality in the United States, 1913–1998." *Quarterly Journal of Economics* 118 (1): 1–39.

Piketty, Thomas, Emmanuel Saez, and Stefanie Stantcheva. 2014. "Optimal Taxation of Top Labor Incomes: A Tale of Three Elasticities." *American Economic Journal: Economic Policy* 6 (1): 230–271.

Saez, Emmanuel, and Gabriel Zucman. 2014. "Wealth Inequality in the United States since 1913: Evidence from Capitalized Income Tax Data." National Bureau of Economic Research, Working Paper No. 20625.

Thaler, Richard, and Cass Sunstein. 2008. *Nudge: Improving Decisions about Health, Wealth, and Happiness.* New Haven, CT: Yale University Press.

CHAPTER SEVEN

Conclusions and Solutions

John H. Cochrane, Lee E. Ohanian, George P. Shultz

Part 1: John H. Cochrane

Why and How We Care about Inequality

Wrapping up a wonderful conference about facts, our panel is supposed to talk about "solutions" to the "problem" of inequality.

We have before us one "solution," the demand from the left for confiscatory income and wealth taxation and a substantial enlargement of the control of economic activity by the state.

Note I don't say "redistribution," though some academics dream about it. We all know there isn't enough money, especially to address real global poverty, and the sad fact is that government checks don't cure poverty. President Obama was refreshingly clear, calling for confiscatory taxation even if it raised no income. "Off with their heads" solves inequality, in a French-Revolution sort of way, and not by using the hair to make wigs for the poor.

The agenda includes a big expansion of spending on government programs, minimum wages, "living wages," government control of wages, especially by minutely divided groups, CEO pay regulation, unions, "regulation" of banks, central direction of all finance, and so on. The logic is inescapable. To "solve inequality," don't just take money from the rich. Stop people, and especially the "wrong" people, from getting rich in the first place.

In this context, I think it is a mistake to accept the premise that inequality, per se, is a "problem" needing to be "solved," and to craft "alternative solutions."

Just why is inequality, per se, a problem?

Suppose a sack of money blows in the room. Some of you get $100, some get $10. Are we collectively better off? If you think "inequality" is a problem, no. We should decline the gift. We should, in fact, take something from people who got nothing, to keep the lucky ones from their $100. This is a hard case to make.

One sensible response is to acknowledge that inequality, by itself, is not a problem. Inequality is a symptom of other problems. I think this is exactly the constructive tone that this conference has taken.

But there are lots of different kinds of inequality, and an enormous variety of different mechanisms at work. Lumping them all together, and attacking the symptom, "inequality," without attacking the problems is a mistake. It's like saying, "Fever is a problem. So medicine shall consist of reducing fevers."

Yes, the reported, pre-tax income and wealth of the top 1 percent in the United States and many other countries has grown. We have an interesting debate whether this is "good" or "market" inequality (Steve Jobs starts a company that invents the iPhone, takes home one-tenth of 1 percent of the welfare—consumer surplus— the iPhone created, and lives in a nice house and flies in a private jet) or "bad," "rent-seeking" inequality, cronyism, exploiting favors from the government. Josh Rauh made a good case for "market." It's interesting how we even use different language. Emmanuel Saez spoke of how much income the 1 percent "get," and Josh how much the 1 percent "earn."

In middle incomes, as Kevin Murphy told us, the "returns to skill" have increased. This has nothing to do with top-end cronyism. As Kevin so nicely reminds us, wages go up when demand for skill goes up *and supply does not.* He locates the supply restriction in awful public schools, taken over by teachers' unions. Limits on high-skill immigration also restrict supply and drive up the skill premium. There's a problem we know how to fix. Confiscatory taxation isn't going to help!

More "education" is one obvious "solution." But we need to be careful here, and not too quickly join the chorus asking that our industry be further subsidized. The returns to education chosen and worked hard for are not necessarily replicated in education subsidized or forced. Free tuition for all majors draws people into art history, too. Forgiving student loans for people who go to nonprofits or government work, or a large increase in wealth and income taxation, remove the market signal to study computer programming rather than art history, which raises the skill premium even more. Saudi Arabia spends a lot on "education" in madrassas around the world. In a Becker memorial conference, remember three rules: supply matters, not just demand; don't redistribute income by distorting prices; and human capital investments respond to incentives. (By the way, I'm all for art history. Just don't pretend that the measured economic returns to education will apply.)

America has a real problem on the lower income end, epitomized by Charles Murray's "Fishtown" (in his book, *Coming Apart: The State of White America, 1960–2010*). A segment of America is stuck in widespread single motherhood, leading to terrible early-child experiences, awful education, substance abuse, and criminality. Seventy percent of male black high school dropouts will end up in prison, hence essentially unemployable and with poor marriage prospects. Less than half are even looking for legal work.

This is a social and economic disaster. And it has nothing to do with whether hedge-fund managers fly private or commercial. It is immune to floods of government cash and, as Casey Mulligan reminded us, government programs are arguably as much of the problem as the solution. So are drug laws, as much of the earlier discussion reminded us.

Around the world, about a billion people still live on $2 a day, have no electricity, drinking water, or even latrines. If you care about "inequality," minimum-wage earners in the US should be *paying* Piketty taxes.

These cases all represent completely different problems. Where there are problems, we should fix them. But we should fix them to fix the problems, not to "reduce inequality."

Kinds of inequality

More puzzling, why are critics on the left so focused on the 1 percent in the US, when by many measures we live in an era of great leveling?

Earnings inequality between men and women has narrowed drastically, as Kevin Murphy reminded us. Inequality *across countries,* and thus across people around the globe, has also been shrinking dramatically even as income inequality within advanced countries has risen. One billion Chinese were rescued from totalitarian misery, and a billion Indians sort-of-rescued from British-style "License-Raj" socialism. These are wonderful events for human progress as well as, incidentally, for global inequality. Sure, these countries have many political and economic problems left, but the "it's all getting worse" story just ain't so.

"Inequality" is about more than income or wealth reported to tax authorities. Consumption is much flatter than income. Rich people mostly give away or reinvest their wealth. It's hard to see just how this is a problem.

Political, social, cultural inequality, inequality of lifespan, of health, of social status, even of schooling are all much flatter than they used to be. (Nick Eberstadt recently summarized these in a nice *Wall Street Journal* op-ed.) Mark Zuckerberg wears a hoodie, not a top hat.

Look at Versailles. Nobody, not even Bill Gates, lives like Marie Antoinette. And nobody in the US lives like her peasants. In 1960, Mao Tse-tung waved his hand and 20 millions died. In 1935, Josef Stalin did the same. Neither reported a lot of income to tax authorities for economists to measure "inequality." It is preposterous to claim that even the citizens of Ferguson, Missouri, with all their problems and injustices, are less equal now than they were in 1950. Or 1850.

Why does it matter at all to a vegetable picker in Fresno, or an unemployed teenager on the south side of Chicago, whether ten or a hundred hedge-fund managers in Greenwich have private jets? How do they even *know* how many hedge-fund managers fly private? They have hard lives, and a lot of problems. But just what problem does top 1 percent inequality really represent to them?

I've been reading Thomas Piketty, Emmanuel Saez, Paul Krugman, Joe Stiglitz, the *New York Times* editorial pages to find the answers. They all recognize that inequality per se is not a persuasive problem, so they must convince us that inequality causes some other social or economic ill.

Here's one. Standard & Poor's economists wrote a recent summary report on inequality, perhaps as penance for downgrading the US debt. They wrote:

> As income inequality increased before the crisis, less affluent households took on more and more debt to keep up—or, in this case, catch up—with the Joneses . . .

In *Vanity Fair*, Joe Stiglitz wrote similarly that inequality is a problem because it causes:

. . . a well-documented lifestyle effect—people outside the
top 1 percent increasingly live beyond their means . . . trickle-down
behaviorism . . .

Aha! Our vegetable picker in Fresno hears that the number of
hedge-fund managers in Greenwich with private jets has doubled.
So, he goes out and buys a pickup truck he can't afford. Therefore, Stiglitz is telling us, we must quash inequality with confiscatory wealth taxation . . . in order to encourage thrift in the lower
classes?

If this argument held any water, wouldn't banning "Keeping up
with the Kardashians" be far more effective? (Or, better, rap music
videos!) If the problem is truly overspending by low-income Americans, can we not think of more directed solutions? For example,
might we not want to remove the enormous taxation of savings
that they face through social programs?

Another example: the S&P report moved on to a new story—
inequality is a problem because rich people save too much of their
money, and poor people don't. So, by transferring money from rich
to poor, we can increase overall consumption and escape "secular
stagnation."

I see. Now the problem is too much saving, not too much
consumption. We need to forcibly transfer wealth from the rich
to the poor in order to overcome our deep problem of national
thriftiness.

I may be bludgeoning the obvious, but let's point out just a few
ways this is incoherent. If Keynesian "spending" and "aggregate
demand" are the problems behind low long-run growth rates—
and that's a big if—standard Keynesian answers are a lot easier
solutions than confiscatory wealth taxation and redistribution.
Which is why standard Keynesians argued for monetary and fiscal
policies, not confiscatory anti-inequality taxation, until the latter
became politically popular.

In a series of recent blog posts, Paul Krugman offers evidence that people vastly underestimate how wealthy the rich are, bemoans how they live separate lives—my fry cook has, in fact, no idea of their lifestyle—and argues for confiscatory taxation to eliminate the "externality" of their *excessive* consumption by the wealthy. Are they consuming too much or too little? Well, I'm glad logical consistency isn't holding back these arguments.

The most common argument is that we have to reduce income inequality to avoid political instability. If we don't redistribute the wealth, the poor will rise up and take it. As a cause-and-effect claim about human affairs, this is dubious amateur political science, one that would look especially amateurish to the political scientists and historians at this Hoover Institution on War, Revolution, and Peace. Maybe the poor should rise up and overthrow the rich, but they never have. Inequality was pretty bad on Thomas Jefferson's farm. But he started a revolution, not his slaves.

These are just three examples, and I won't go on since time is short. But there are some interesting patterns. The answer is always the same—confiscatory wealth taxation and expansion of the state. The "problem" this answer is supposed to solve keeps changing. When an actual economic problem is adduced—excessive spending by the poor, inadequate spending by the rich, political instability—they don't advocate the problem's natural solution. These "problems" are being thought up afterward to justify the desired answer. And amazing, novel, and undocumented cause-and-effect assertions about public policy are dreamed up and passed around like Internet cat videos.

Politics and money

But these are serious people. Let's recognize this is all the balderdash and distraction that it seems, and that we are circling around the elephant in the room. Let's try to find the core issue that they are really talking about. Let's find a common ground, a resolvable difference, so we can stop talking past each other.

In the end, most of these authors are pretty clear about the real problem they see: money and politics. They worry that too much money is corrupting politics, and they want to take away the money to purify the politics.

That explains the obsessive focus on the income and wealth of the top 1 percent. Consumption may be flatter, but income and wealth buy political connections. And all of our concern about the status of the poor, the returns to skill, awful education, the effects of widespread incarceration, all this is irrelevant to the money-and-politics nexus.

Now, the critique of an increasingly rent-seeking society echoes from both the Left and the libertarians. Rent-seeking is a big problem. Cronyism is a big problem. George Stigler finds a lot to agree with in Joe Stiglitz. As do Milton Friedman, James Buchanan, and so forth.

But now comes the most astounding lack of logic of all. If the central problem is rent-seeking—abuse of the power of the state—to deliver economic goods to the wealthy and politically powerful, how in the world is *more government* the answer?

If we increase the statutory maximum federal income tax rate 70 percent, on top of state and local taxes, estate taxes, payroll taxes, corporate taxes, sales taxes, and on and on—at a Becker conference, always add up all the taxes, not just the one you want to raise and pretend the others are zero—will that not simply, dramatically, *increase* the demand for tax lawyers, lobbyists, and loopholes?

If you believe cronyism is the problem, why is the first item on your agenda not to repeal the Dodd-Frank act and Obamacare, surely two of the biggest invitations to cronyism of our lifetimes? And move on to the rotten energy section of the corporate tax code.

They don't, and here I think lies the important and resolvable difference. Stiglitz wrote that "wealth is a main determinant of power." Stigler might answer, no, power is a main determinant of wealth. To Stiglitz, if the state grabs all the wealth, even if that wealth is fairly won, then the state can ignore rent-seeking and benevolently exercise its power on behalf of the common man. Stigler would say that government power inevitably invites rent-seeking. His solution to cronyism is to limit the government's ability to hand out goodies in the first place. We want a simple, transparent, fair, flat, and low tax system.

Here is where I think Josh Rauh's masterful collection of data—that the upper 1 percent in the US are making their money fairly—falls flat to Left ears. They think even *fairly* gotten money will pervert politics.

Now we have boiled the argument down to a simple question of cause and effect. They believe that raising tax rates and a large increase in state direction of economic activity will *reduce* rent-seeking and cronyism. I assert the opposite, which is the rather traditional conclusion of the vast literature on public choice as well as obvious experience. If I were trying to be polite, I might say it's an interesting new theory to be debated and investigated. But I'm not, and it isn't. It is the cream on the crop of amateur ad-hoc assertions of cause-and-effect relationships in human affairs, changing the *sign* of everything we know.

As we look around the world, cronyism, rent-seeking—using the power of the state to deliver riches to yourself and privilege to your family—is a huge problem, not just driving inequality, but driving most of poverty, lack of growth, and human misery throughout the world. But Egypt, say, does not suffer because it is *not good enough* at grabbing wealth, stifling markets, and blocking the rise of entrepreneurs. Quite the opposite.

China and India did not start growing by confiscatory taxation of income and wealth and increasing state intervention in markets. Exactly the opposite. And the parts of the world left or falling behind—parts of the Middle East, Latin America (think Venezuela), parts of Africa—have just nothing to do with the private-jet purchases of US hedge-fund billionaires.

Politics and the agenda

But let's go with their argument. At least now the argument makes sense, in a way that limiting envy-induced spend-thriftery does not. But looked at in the light of day, the argument is truly scary. They are saying that the government must confiscate individual wealth so that individual wealth cannot influence politics in directions they don't like. Koch brothers, no. Public employee unions, yes.

We finally agree on a cause-and-effect proposition. Yes, expanding the power of the state to direct economic activity and strip people of wealth is a well-proven way to cement the power of the state and quash dissent.

So now you see why I rebel at the presumption that "inequality" is a problem, and why I rebel at the task of articulating an alternative "solution." "Inequality" has become a meaningless buzzword, or code word for "on our team," like "sustainability," or "social justice." Should we discuss "free-market solutions" to address "social justice?"

"Inequality" has become a code word for endless, thoughtless, and counterproductive intrusions into economic activity. Minimum wages, stronger teachers' unions, even prison guard unions, are all advocated on the grounds of "providing middle-class jobs" to "reduce inequality," though they do the opposite. Mayor Bill de Blasio has already reduced it to farce. As reported in the *New York Times,* the latest energy efficiency standards for fancy New York high-rises are being put in place. Why? To cool the planet by a billionth of a degree? To stem the rise of the oceans by a nanometer? No, first on the list . . . to reduce inequality. Poor people pay more of their incomes in heating bills, you see.

Finally, why is "inequality" so strongly on the political agenda right now? Here I am not referring to academics. Kevin has been studying the skill premium for thirty years. Emmanuel likewise has devoted his career to important measurement questions, and will do so whether or not the *New York Times* editorial page cheers. All of economics has been studying various poverty traps for a generation, as represented well by the other authors at this conference. Why is there a big *political* debate just now? Why are the administration and its allies in the punditry, such as Paul Krugman and Joe Stiglitz, all atwitter about "inequality?" Why are otherwise generally sensible institutions like the IMF [International Monetary Fund], the S&P, and even the IPCC [Intergovernmental Panel on Climate Change] jumping on the "inequality" bandwagon?

That answer seems pretty clear. Because they don't want to talk about Obamacare, Dodd-Frank, bailouts, debt, the stimulus, the rotten cronyism of energy policy, denial of education to the poor and to minorities, the abject failure of their policies to help poor and middle-class people, and especially sclerotic growth. Restarting a centuries-old fight about "inequality" and "tax the rich," class envy resurrected from a Huey Long speech in the 1930s, is like throwing a puppy into a third grade math class that isn't going well. You know you will make it to the bell.

That observation, together with the obvious incoherence of ideas the political inequality writers bring us, leads me to a happy thought that this too will pass, and once a new set of talking points emerges we can go on to something else.

But if that is our circumstance, clearly we should not fall for the trap. Don't surrender the agenda. State our own agenda. We care about prosperity. We care about fixing the real, serious, economic problems our country faces and especially that people on the bottom of society face. Globally, we care about the billion on $2 a day that no amount of tax and transfer will help.

The "solutions," the secrets of prosperity, are simple and old-fashioned: property rights, rule of law, honest government, economic and political freedom. A decent government, yes, providing decent roads, schools, and laws necessary for the common good. Confiscatory taxation and extensive government direction of economic activity are simply not on the list.

Part 2: Lee E. Ohanian

My view is that inequality is not an issue that policy should address. Some have argued that policy should redistribute income away from the highest earners. This view is counterproductive, as it does not sufficiently recognize that our top earners create enormous surpluses for society. Bill Gates at Microsoft, Steve Jobs at Apple, Fred Smith at FedEx, Sam Walton of Wal-Mart, and many others who started new businesses have directly and indirectly created millions of new jobs, created new industries, and transformed our society. And these individuals have received only a tiny fraction of the economic value that they have created.

Society, however, should care about economic opportunities for the lowest earners. I therefore will focus my remarks on expanding opportunities and raising the productivity of these workers. I want to focus on the lowest earners for two reasons. One is because for the last thirty to forty years, workers with low levels of human capital have been swimming upstream against technology. My work with [Per] Krusell, [José-Víctor] Rios-Rull, and [Giovanni] Violante, and the work of Kevin Murphy and others, indicates that technological improvements over this period are complements to highly skilled workers, raising their marginal productivity, but are substitutes for low-skilled workers, reducing their marginal productivity. This means that increasingly sophisticated technologies that keep making capital goods better and cheaper will continue to place downward pressure on the wages and opportunities of the lowest earners.

The second reason I will focus on the lowest-income workers is that many of our policies toward lower earners are schizophrenic. On the one hand, we have policies now that provide much larger transfers to the lowest earners today than they did in the past. For example, a family of four at the poverty level has about $22,300 per year of pre-tax income. Consumption for that same family of four on average, however, is about $44,000 per year, which means that their consumption level is about twice as high as their income. But consider the relationship between consumption and income among poverty-level families prior to LBJ's Great Society initiatives in 1964. At this time, a family of four at the poverty level was consuming only about 10 percent in excess of their income. We're certainly providing many more resources to low-earning families today. But on the other hand, we have policies in place that either limit economic opportunities for low earners and/distort the incentives for those earners to achieve prosperity.

I'm going to focus on K-12 education and immigration policy as areas of reform that in my view would expand economic opportunities for low earners as well as increase their productivity and skills.

I will focus on introducing competition into K-12 education as an important reform for increasing student skills and performance. I will begin with some statistics on student math achievement, which have been produced by Eric Hanushek of the Hoover Institution. The statistics are grim and paint a dismal picture of how we are preparing many US students for careers, particularly those from low-income households. The Organization for Economic Cooperation and Development (OECD) administers the Program for International Student Assessment test (PISA). It's given to about half a million students between fifteen and sixteen years old, in forty-four countries. Thirty-four of those are OECD countries, which are the advanced, high-income countries, including Canada, and the countries of Western Europe.

The US does not perform well in this assessment. US fifteen- and sixteen-year-olds rank thirty-fourth out of all forty-four countries, and the US is twenty-seventh out of the thirty-four OECD countries. Our proficiency rate in math is only 32 percent. Only five states have a proficiency rate of 40 percent or higher: two large states, Massachusetts and New Jersey, and three small states, Kansas, North Dakota, and Vermont. Proficiency in California is just 24 percent, which is worse than Kazakhstan. New York's proficiency is at 30 percent. The US proficiency rate is particularly low for minorities. It is 11 percent for African Americans and it is 15 percent for Hispanics.

Low US performance is not simply due to the fact that our student population is more heterogeneous than some other countries. Comparing the top achiever in this international assessment, which is Shanghai, China, with our best state, which is Massachusetts, shows a difference in math achievement that is equivalent to two full years of education. American students on average clearly do not have sufficient math aptitude.

To learn more about this, I examined representative questions from the PISA test. There are six levels of questions. A representative level two question is recognizing that two-fourths and five-tenths are the same number within a one-sentence word problem. Twenty-five percent of US students are not proficient at level two math. PISA test developers define level two proficiency as being able to be self-sufficient in terms of being able to understand common transactions. Level three questions involve rank-ordering numbers with decimal points. Forty percent of US students are not proficient at level three. Just 2 percent of fifteen- and sixteen-year-old US students are proficient at level six. A representative level six question involves using the familiar distance/time/rate formula, within a sentence. For example, "Helen rode her bike five kilometers and it took her fifteen minutes. On the way home, she took a shortcut, which involved a four kilometer ride, and it took her thirteen minutes. Calculate the average speed on Helen's trip." Only 2 percent of our fifteen- to sixteen-year-olds can answer this question. This level of math proficiency is simply unacceptable, and current US performance statistics mean that many of our children will not be competitive for jobs involving quantitative and logical skills that extend beyond the most basic levels.

Low math performance by US students is not due to insufficient spending on K-12 education. In fact, we spend more per pupil than almost any country. Our spending per pupil is twice as much as the Slovak Republic, which outperforms us, as do Estonia, Vietnam, Slovenia, and the Czech Republic. These are all low-income non-OECD countries in the PISA assessment that do not spend nearly as much on K-12 education as the US.

Improving K-12 education requires introducing competition in this process, including teacher tenure reform, which will make it feasible to replace the worst-performing teachers. Nationwide, the dismissal rate for teachers is 0.1 percent. In California, the dismissal rate is even lower than that, with about two dismissals per year out of 275,000 K-12 teachers, which is about .0008 percent. To put this in perspective, dismissal rates across occupations range from about 3 percent to about 9 percent per year, depending upon age, education, and occupation.

Dismissal rates in K-12 are so low because the process can cost up to $250,000 per case due to costly litigation, and the dismissal process can take several years. Dismissal protection and seniority-based layoff procedures are endemic in teacher union contracts, and they substantially impact teaching quality by protecting the worst-performing teachers. A recent lawsuit filed by nine California schoolchildren, Vergara v. California, argued that many students are receiving deficient educations because of ineffective teachers. The court agreed, and found that seniority-based layoffs and teacher tenure were unconstitutional. The court noted that "the evidence on grossly ineffective teachers is compelling, and indeed shocking."

Ineffective teachers are an important reason why some students are not able to succeed. Eric Hanushek of the Hoover Institution finds that if the bottom 8 percent of teachers were replaced with the average of the truncated distribution, then math and science scores in the US would rise substantially. He estimates present discounted value of about $100 trillion in increased national income. Others, including Raj Chetty, now at Stanford, have estimated similar gains.

A teacher who is one standard deviation above the mean in terms of effectiveness generates marginal gains of about $400,000 in present value of student earnings. If kids are lucky enough to have a ninetieth percentile teacher, they can expect about a $900,000 PDV (present discounted value) gain in future incomes relative to having a median teacher. The value of a good teacher is enormous.

The second aspect of introducing competitive pressure in K-12 education is merit-based pay. Teacher salaries are typically set by rigid schedules that depend upon seniority and the number of degrees held by the teacher. Typically, there are no salary differences across teaching areas, and salary doesn't depend on effort or performance. This salary policy distorts incentives and guarantees shortages by teaching areas like math and science. The Los Angeles Unified School District is estimated to pay about $500 million per year in salary to teachers with additional degrees that have zero correlation with improved teaching performance.

Union compensation policies are also distorting the incentives to become teachers and are resulting in fewer highly capable individuals pursuing teaching as a career. Caroline Hoxby of Hoover and Andrew Lee find that there has been a significant decrease in the number of high-ability individuals who enter teaching, as a consequence of wage compression and the lack of merit-based pay. They find that those in the bottom 25 percent of the SAT distribution now make up about 40 percent of K-12 teachers. And they find that much of this change in composition is due to wage compression, reflecting these types of salary schedules.

The policy recommendation is straightforward. Introduce competition into K-12 education. Reform teacher tenure and adopt merit-based pay. Don't protect the poorest performing teachers. Pay the best teachers very well. Pay teaching specialists, such as math and science teachers, according to relative scarcity. To improve student achievement, we need to reward the best teachers and provide incentives for highly skilled and ambitious individuals to enter the teaching profession. I anticipate that these reforms will significantly contribute to enabling our children to become skilled in math and logical thinking, and to develop the necessary quantitative skills to be competitive in a labor market that is changing almost continuously in response to advances in technology.

The second policy reform I will discuss is immigration reform. Reforming immigration for high-skilled workers and entrepreneurs is necessary to increase new business formation. As we all know, macroeconomic performance continues to be weak. The employment-to-population ratio is down by about 7 percent relative to its 2007 level, and business sector labor productivity growth, which has averaged 2.5 percent per year from the late 1940s until recently, is now growing at 0.9 percent per year since mid-2009.

I cannot overstate the importance and severity of this productivity growth shortfall. Historically, the US doubled labor productivity in the business sector every twenty-eight years. At its current growth rate of 0.9 percent per year, however, it will take roughly seventy-two years to double. We need to increase business start-ups and entrepreneurship because new business creation is fundamental for job creation and for increasing productivity. The new business creation rate is down 35 percent from the 1980s, with much of this decline coming in the last ten years. The start-up rate in every state, even North Dakota, which is experiencing a boom in energy production, has declined substantially.

New businesses are a key factor in the process of economic growth because thirty years from now, the biggest employers will likely be the start-ups from today or from the recent past. Half of the Fortune 500 list of the biggest companies turns over roughly every ten years. This is a symptom of the fact that all businesses have a life cycle, in which even the most successful ultimately stop growing. This means that creating a persistently growing economy requires a persistent flow of successful new businesses. To get a sense of just how important start-ups are, note that in most years the economy actually loses jobs on net if you take out job creation by start-ups. In terms of gross job creation, start-ups and young, high-growth firms account for nearly two-thirds of job creation. And in terms of productivity growth, start-ups are responsible for many of our most important innovations, including the airplane, automobiles, air conditioning, the computer, electrification, railroads, refrigeration, the telephone, and many Internet applications.

The question is: who's going to be the next Intel, the next Microsoft, the next Amgen, the next Oracle, or the next Apple? There is no reason to think that our economy will improve significantly, or that opportunities for low earners will improve significantly, unless we increase the number of start-ups.

Immigration reform is important for developing more new businesses. US immigration restrictions make it difficult for skilled foreign nationals to stay here. We have many foreign nationals who are ambitious, skilled, talented people, and who would like to stay in the United States. But we make it difficult for them to remain. Half of all successful high-technology start-ups are founded or co-founded by an immigrant. Forty percent of the Fortune 500 were founded by an immigrant or by the child of an immigrant. Intel, Google, and Yahoo are recent examples.

In the high technology area, most immigrant start-ups are from China or India. And yet we have country-specific quotas on immigrants, some of which date back to the 1980s. The problem is so severe that there is a start-up incubator called Blueseed which was planning to purchase an ocean liner, have it docked twelve miles off of San Francisco port in international waters, and have it house about 1,500 entrepreneurs who would get in skiffs and come to Silicon Valley and stay as long as they can in accordance with immigration rules. Then they will go back to the Blueseed boat. This highlights the importance of restricting high-skilled immigration. By expanding high-skilled immigration, we will increase start-ups, which in turn will increase job creation and productivity growth, and expand opportunities for low earners.

The lowest earners need more human capital to increase their skills and productivity, and a healthier economy with more job creation. Reforming K-12 education policies through competition, and expanding new business creation by allowing immigrant entrepreneurs to remain in the US, will help our lowest earners succeed.

Part 3: George P. Shultz

I am also going to focus on the low end of the distribution and talk particularly about people who are trying to do something about getting people out of poverty. But let me make a couple of remarks first.

There has been reference a couple of times to the fact that the huge increase in prosperity in China has lifted lots of people out of poverty, and that's attributed to Chinese policy. Let me recall a remark made to me by Deng Xiaoping in the early 1980s. We were meeting and talking about this and he said, "Well, China's ready for the two openings." I said, "What are they?" He said, "Well, the first opening is inside China, and we're going to make it possible for people to move around more and seek good opportunities." I said, "What's the second opening?" And he said, "The second opening is to the outside world, and I'm glad there's a reasonably coherent world to open up to."

In other words, he realized that with a tremendous amount of leadership from the United States, there had been created in the world an economic and security commons that everybody benefited from. I might note that nowadays that commons is coming apart at the seams. And it's one of the factors that's going to make it hard for what happened in China to be duplicated.

The other question I have is on the top end, and I ask the John Taylors and John Cochranes of this world, who know all about the Fed, what it does and why. Why are they working so hard to increase inequality by jacking up the income of the wealthy? After all, with this gusher of liquidity they've produced, as far as I can see, they're pushing on a string as far as the real economy is concerned and they're pumping up asset prices like mad. So they seem to have a determined policy of increasing inequality. What's going on here, anyway? Is this a government program of some sort? [Laughter]

You're laughing. I'm crying. [Laughter]

Well, my first example of a person who's really trying to work at the problems of the poor is Muhammad Yunus, and you probably all know him. He's a Bangladeshi who got some economic education at Vanderbilt, went back to Bangladesh, and noticed that poor people who were trying to get something going paid huge interest rates. So he started micro-lending mostly to women who could buy sewing machines or other things and start little businesses. In a sense, they would use entrepreneurship to get themselves out of poverty with these small loans.

This has spread around now. It's the kind of thing that is scalable. There are quite a few Grameen Banks in the United States and they're in various other countries. It's a way of helping people get out of poverty by exercising their own efforts and ingenuity. It seems to me this is a really good development. And I'm interested in the fact that Muhammad has now decided, having been banker for the poor, to be the health care provider for the poor.

So what is he doing? Apparently there are several of these clinics in Bangladesh now, but I know of at least one starting in the United States as an experiment. Yunus is creating clinics located in poor areas, and he's realizing that one of the reasons people stay poor is that they have bad health. If they were healthier, they would have a better chance of getting along. So he puts the clinic in a poor area and people can become members of the clinic. He says, "You cannot give them membership; they must pay something, even if it's an IOU, because if you give it to them, they won't put any value on it. But if they put even an IOU in, at least they're acknowledging psychologically that this is a thing of value."

What are these clinics? Well, there are doctors and nurses, but most of the people in them are called coaches who coach their clients to move toward a lifestyle that the doctors and the nurses think they should have—things like stopping smoking and walking around the block once in a while. At least in the early returns from Bangladesh, people are getting healthier. We'll see what happens in this country. I think it's a very interesting insight. Part of the problems the poor have stem from their health, and this is a way of getting at it. It's a matter of lifestyle, and improved lifestyle will improve health.

So that's one example of somebody working at this problem. I don't know to what extent it's been studied, but I think it's worth looking at because, anecdotally, it's done a lot of good and has some real prospects.

The other person is completely different, and the scalability is harder, maybe impossible, although something is beginning to happen. This is something in San Francisco called Delancey Street.

Many of you may be familiar with it. It is run by a woman named Mimi Silbert—a tiny, dynamic woman. She says, "You people at Stanford try to pick the best people to come to Stanford. I pick the worst people to come to Delancey Street: criminals, murderers, the worst." She interviews every person. They have to want to come to Delancey Street. That's the only requirement.

At Delancey Street, the doors are not locked from the inside. If you want to go out, you can go out, but the doors lock once you have left. You can't get back in again. The residents, as she calls them (not inmates), do everything to make Delancey Street work. If you try to give Mimi money as a philanthropist, she won't take it because, she says, "Our object at Delancey Street is to make sure our residents, no matter how they come in, leave with the equivalent of a high school degree, a marketable skill, and an attitude that, 'I can make it legitimately in the real world if I get a crack at it.' That's the object."

So she says, "I have to run an organization the same way. Delancey Street has to be self-supporting." They run a moving service, they run a good restaurant, and they make enough money to support themselves. You go into Delancey Street and the place is absolutely spotless. She makes sure the residents keep it clean. And it is a success because they graduate residents who make it in the real world. They start with the bottom of the pile, not the top of the pile.

It's hard to replicate because there's only one Mimi Silbert, but there are now five or six semi-replications. She's not satisfied with them. She was telling me the other day, "Some of the people running them insist on getting paid. You can't have that. You've got to live like everybody else." She lives in Delancey Street and she eats the same food the residents do and she's there all the time, so she's part of it. And it is interesting to see how this tiny little woman (I don't know if she's even five feet tall) has hulking big murderers shaking in front of her and doing what she wants. This is heroic, and I should think some of her ideas ought to get into our prisons so that when people come out, maybe they're a little better.

Right now, when some young kid is caught with minor possession of some drug, he gets thrown in jail, and that's where he learns to be a real criminal. By the time he comes out, you have a problem on your hands. It doesn't make sense. A lot of these drug-related convicts shouldn't be there in the first place, in my opinion. But at any rate, I should think we could do a better job in our jails of working with people and turning people like Mimi loose on the jails.

In a sense, these examples are not about economics. You're not playing with supply and demand. You're saying, "Here is a person who sees a problem and takes it on." And the message I get is that you can do something about these problems if you're willing to work at them and have people who are motivated enough to give it a good try.

I go along completely with Eric Hanushek's notion that you have to introduce more choice into education. Certainly K-12 education is a huge problem, as you brought out. The statistics are appalling in this country. And I think it's the case that the Alliance for School Choice is beginning to make some headway. Milton's foundation (Friedman Foundation for Educational Choice) has been working at this, of course, and has long advocated vouchers. Vouchers have become a bad word. The current administration has sued Louisiana for using vouchers to move some kids into a better school. I don't know what in the world explains that lawsuit, but vouchers are a way to improve education. Giving tax advantages for paying tuition is one way, and there are lots of other ways in which school choice is being expanded.

I have some fun with Governor Brown about once a year. When he was mayor of Oakland, he started something called the Oakland Military Institute. I helped him along the way, and it was clear that he had a terrible time getting it established. The education bureaucracy tried to block it. It was only because he was a former governor that finally he was able to get it into being. He has a luncheon every year and usually I'm one of the speakers. I say to him, "Jerry, you have seen how hard it is to get choice through the bureaucracy. I want to congratulate you on beating the bureaucracy and getting this thing into effect. And you also know that every student in this school comes here as a matter of choice. Nobody has to come here. And the school knows that unless it is attractive to students, nobody will come." And so they graduate practically everybody. They go on to college. It's a great thing.

So I say, "Governor, why can't you spread this around a little bit in California?" It's hard. Do you know why it's hard? The teachers' union has elected everybody and so those elected have a hard time bucking them. So I think the root of our problem is political.

We had an initiative on the ballot put there by Arnold Schwarzenegger. You get tenure in a California school after you're there for two years—just two years. We had an initiative on the ballot to change it to four years. That's still ridiculous. The teachers' union beat it, hands down. There's a lot of power there. So somehow we've got to face up to this.

I have one final piece of experience that is my way of saying programmatically that you can do things. Way back in my career I used to be a labor economist. And when I was at the University of Chicago, the late Al Rees and I worried about unemployment in the ghetto and what could be done about it. For some reason, that became known in Washington and I found myself invited to the White House. Lyndon Johnson was also worried about this problem and he had White House task forces to work on subjects that were not secret, but they were quiet and private—small things.

So he asked me to chair a task force on this problem and I agreed to do it. Then he says to me, "George, if you come up with a good idea and it turns out to be your idea, it's probably not going to go very far. But if that idea turns out to be *my* idea, it just might go somewhere. Am I making myself clear?" [Laughter]

So we had a good task force with some good staff from the Labor Department, and we did a lot of work. We came up with a good idea and President Johnson took it and ran with it very effectively. The essence of the idea was that you're never going to get anywhere trying to use training programs for these people. Many of them don't even know how to be in the labor force. So you have to create a situation where they go to a place of employment and get trained and oriented to a specific job. So we got Henry Ford to chair a big employer group, and somebody said to him, "How are you going to get companies to cooperate?" He said, "All our suppliers will cooperate."

Anyway, it spread all over the country and it did a lot of good work for quite a long while. These things have a tendency to peter out after a while, but nevertheless, they show you that things can be done. And in terms of training programs, one of the things that was clear from this is that if you link a training program to a specific job setting, you're much better off. You're going to get somewhere and maybe have a chance that it will work.

JOHN TAYLOR: We've had a lot of suggestions, a lot of solutions, some more difficult than others. These extraordinary inspiring examples—you referred to Muhammad Yunus and San Francisco—are intriguing.

I worked for President George W. Bush, and also [George] H. W. Bush. And there was this idea of a thousand points of light. And the idea was that somehow you could get more people interested in the kinds of things you're talking about. But it doesn't really happen that much. So I keep thinking, what would you do to generate more of that? It may be that some of our programs crowd that activity out, but I'm sure if you asked these people, they would say, "No, we want more of those programs." So the question is, what do you do, George, to get more of what you're talking about?

GEORGE SHULTZ: Well, I think the Muhammad Yunus model, that's scalable. You can have micro-lending and it is spreading. And if this health care notion works, it makes common sense. That's scalable, too. In fact, I think you might even try to apply it to education, and getting people in school and keeping them in school and so on, this notion of coaches. Because often the basic problem is the home. And if you can somehow provide coaches in that model, perhaps you can get somewhere. So I think that's scalable.

The Mimi Silbert side is harder because she's such a driver on the one hand, but nevertheless, the ideas are there: that it's possible to take these people who have terrible records and turn them around and get them to at least a high school level and get them with a skill of some kind so they can sell it when they get out in the world. Otherwise, when you get out of jail, what happens? They give you $200 and send you off with no skills and you have no chance of getting a job. So what happens? Criminality happens. So there's an idea here that if we work at it hard enough, perhaps we can move.

QUESTION: *Thanks. Great session. I really appreciated all the presentations. We heard a lot about the need for public school reform. That part of our human capital development process is broken and we need to fix it. I'm thoroughly on board with that and I like the ideas I heard, about increasing choice and competitive pressure. But there is another part of our human capital development process in the United States that has become increasingly broken, and that is the opportunities for less-educated, less-credentialed people to develop their human capital once they're in the labor market.*

So in a number of respects, the labor market has become a less hospitable place in the United States over time for people who enter with less education. Kevin Murphy made the point that the kinds of jobs that those people traditionally held have diminished, but I think there's something else that has happened as well. We talked about the expanse of occupational licensing. That's hugely expanded in the United States, which makes it more difficult for less educated people to enter certain jobs that they might find attractive.

But there are many other things that have happened as well. There's been an erosion of the employment-at-will doctrine over time in the United States. There's been an expansion in the protected classes of workers based on age, race, gender, and so on. These things make employers more cautious in their hiring decisions, more reluctant to take chances on people who have a spotty record, limited educational background. There's been an enormous expansion of imprisonment rates in certain demographic groups, less-educated black men. It's quite extraordinary.

You put all that together with the fact that it has become easier technologically for employers over time to screen people out because of the information revolution, the expansion of data, on everything from contact with the criminal justice system, spotty credit records, and so on. And it has become much harder for people who either were not suited for learning through education in the first place, or had the misfortune to be stuck in one of these lousy public school education systems, to acquire human capital, and by learning by doing on the job, that kind of thing. This is related to declining fluidity and entrepreneurship in the labor market.

If you look across states over time, you see the states in which measures of entrepreneurship and fluidity in the labor market have declined the most. Those are the same states where you see the biggest declines in employment rates among less-educated workers and younger workers. So I think that part of our human capital development process is also in serious need of repair.

SHULTZ: Well, I agree with your point. So there are a lot of different kinds of things that can be done. I don't want to get into the whole drug issue, but we could change our policy toward drugs, to great advantage I believe, and start focusing more on how to persuade people not to take them and so on. Focus on that, rather than the war on drugs and throwing them in jail. So that's a whole big other issue.

Personally, I think the community college system is a really important system. It's not been getting the kind of funding it deserves lately, and community colleges that work closely with the employer base, as I think most of them do, can do a great deal in this area.

OHANIAN: It seems that the California Correctional Peace Officers Association, which is the union that represents prison guards, is a huge impediment to reforming inmates. California used to be among the top three in the United States in terms of recidivism. Today we're dead last, or close to it, and when you look at the political positions taken by the California prison guards association, as George noted, we have a three-strikes law, which places many nonviolent offenders in prison for close to life sentences.

I have a personal experience with this. My gardener in LA, whom I've had for fifteen years, is a Mexican immigrant. He's close to seventy, and is a self-made guy. He owns two six-unit apartment buildings in Santa Monica, which makes him wealthier than many of us in this room. He still gardens. His oldest son is in prison. He was caught three times for selling marijuana. My gardener spent $150,000 in legal fees to defend him. He gets out in eighteen years. Every time a potential revision to the three-strikes law comes up, it's fought tooth and nail by the California prison guards association, because it means fewer jobs for California prison guards. But locking up nonviolent marijuana dealers in prison for two decades doesn't seem to make much sense.

It's their market, and many of these prison guards are paid six-figure salaries. When you look at prison guard salaries, California stands way out, at about $90,000 per year. New Jersey is around $70,000 and then the other salaries for prison guards are more in line with other police officer salaries. And Arnold Schwarzenegger, when he was governor, was so upset about this that he was not able to agree on a new contract with the prison guards' union. And if a new contract can't be formulated, then the existing contract simply rolls over.

And then quickly after earning office, maybe George can comment on this, Governor Brown quickly agreed to a new contract with the California prison guards association. And virtually every newspaper in the state took issue with Brown's capitulation despite the fact that most major newspapers in this state tend to be politically liberal newspapers. In some sense there's a direct fix here that would help us substantially, in terms of incarceration.

SHULTZ: The phenomenon of automatic deduction of union dues and having to be a member of the union means the flow to the unions is just gigantic. I remember in the old days when I used to work in the labor relations field. There was a wonderful guy that everybody looked to, a leader who really knew what was on the rank and file. They wanted to have the check-off and he opposed it. He said, "No, I don't want to check off. I want to go around and collect dues from my members, one by one. Because there's no time like when a guy's giving you some money that he's willing to tell you what's on his mind." And that was why he was so much better informed than everybody else. But now they all want the check-off. And they have it.

QUESTION: *Do I recall correctly that there is a sort of sad epilogue to the Grameen Bank story, that the Bangladesh government charged Yunus and forced him out of the bank that he had created? And what was the political dynamic that brought about that kind of outcome, if you know?*

SHULTZ: From what I understand, they're so jealous of Muhammad and his popularity and his Nobel Prize and so on, they're doing everything they can to knock him down. And so they've said, "You're too old to be in your bank," and so he can't be chairman of his bank anymore. Nevertheless, the idea continues to spread.

QUESTION: *I've been reading a little bit about the launch of the war on poverty fifty years ago, when President Lyndon Johnson invoked Abraham Lincoln as inspiring him. So John, I want to ask you this question. He said the marker that they would use to measure success in the war on poverty was the unemployment rate for teenagers who were African American males. And he said, "Look how much higher this unemployment rate was." And I think it was maybe—I don't want to get the number wrong—let's say it was 24 percent, which was 10 percent higher than it was for other American teenage males.*

And you know that rate now is quite high. So why is the minimum wage still considered a good idea, when the people who lose jobs because of the minimum wage, it seems to me, are these high school kids, who maybe don't have a lot of skills, who've got a functional illiteracy rate of 20 percent, and they can't get a basic job because they're blocked? Is that something you see as fixable, and am I alone in thinking that's a problem?

COCHRANE: Not just the unemployment rate, but the employment-to-population ratio, the labor force participation rate is truly tragic. It went exactly the wrong way. And I think that's the problem of not defining what we're talking about in inequality. You end up saying silly things. You end up with, "We need to raise minimum wages to help poor people." But it doesn't help people who don't have jobs, and so it is unlikely to flatten inequality. That's why I objected so much to just using the term without defining it. It gets used as this vague buzzword for whatever's on your mind today.

OHANIAN: Even if you look at the employment rate of sixteen- to nineteen-year-olds, it's crashed since the economy went south in 2008. In 2000, the employment rate of sixteen- to nineteen-year-olds was 44 percent. Today it's 21 percent. The young people are the ones who've really been impacted by a weak economy.

QUESTION: *I know nothing about labor economics, but I've looked at some numbers and I've never gotten anyone to give me a straight answer to the numbers. And I'm not good at remembering numbers, but it's something like 10 million undocumented workers and 10 million high school dropouts in the labor force. And I ask, does this have an effect on the earnings of high school dropouts? And the answer I usually get is, "I don't know," or, "Yes, people have studied that, but the effect is very small." So I'll ask it to this august group.*

SHULTZ: Well, if you are trying to run a farm, you have a hell of a time hiring anybody but an immigrant. I think something like 80 percent of the people working on US farms are immigrants because they're the only ones who will take those jobs. Ask a caterer in San Francisco. A lot of big events go on in San Francisco, where lots of people come and caterers put on the meals. And they'll tell you that you can't hire anybody in San Francisco because they're all on unemployment compensation. They'd rather be on unemployment compensation than take a job with a caterer. If you take a job with a caterer, you're going to work. It's much better to be on unemployment compensation. So I think there are some real problems. And immigration is not one of them.

OHANIAN: If you go back to those proficiency statistics, 25 percent of fifteen- to sixteen-year-olds don't recognize two-fourths and five-tenths are the same number. That's probably going to be disproportionately the group that are high school dropouts. So these are people who have very few marketable skills. So

I suspect, whether there are a lot of low-skilled immigrants or not, these are people that are going to be struggling.

COCHRANE: My impression of the numbers is that there is an effect. But it's small because, as George mentioned colorfully, there's not that much substitution between domestic and immigrant low-skilled labor. High-skilled immigrants are very good for low-skilled Americans because they're complements, not substitutes.

And a point Kevin made which I thought was very good—supply and demand. If you can help some low-skilled Americans escape into high skill, that lowers the numbers of low-skilled Americans left and therefore will raise the wages to those who are left. I think the bottom line in empirical literature is that low-skilled immigration isn't that much of a substitute, and high-skilled immigration would help them a lot.

QUESTION: *A couple of quick points. Number one, surely we have too many people in prison for the three-strikes stuff and minor drug offenses and so on. But California spends more per incarcerated inmate than the after-tax take-home pay of a median American family. So the spending isn't primarily on the prison guards. That's a part of it, but the whole prison-industrial complex is a sinkhole and disaster. We need to incarcerate some people but, you know, the recidivism's high.*

The second point I was going to say is that there's been a lot of focus, refocus, on early childhood interventions, before school. We've had fits and starts with Head Start, not to try to create a pun or anything. And the evaluation of it has come and gone. For a while it looked like it might have worked, then it didn't really. And people are arguing about that now. Jim Heckman has this place in the Midwest with a specific intervention that he thinks is the silver bullet. So I'm just wondering if any of you guys have thought about any of those things and if you have anything to add to my kind of very simplistic summary of the literature.

SHULTZ: I'd just put Mimi in charge of the prison system.

OHANIAN: I would add something on early childhood intervention. Look at Fishtown, as described by Charles Murray's book *Coming Apart.* You're looking at 70 percent, 80 percent, 90 percent single mothers. So if you have a poor, uneducated, single mother, you're just at a horrible cognitive disadvantage and essentially having the federal government trying to bring up small children instead of a married couple. I'd rather think about where that problem came from. It didn't used to be that way.

QUESTION: *This may be partly a plea, but I'm struck because the title of the conference is inequality, and what you've been talking about correctly is poverty. And it seems to be that one way that might start making the conversation a little better is to be very clear that what we're concerned about is the low-income folks and giving them better opportunities, and improving education to help this stuff, and we're much less concerned about whether that low-income bracket gets X percent or X + 1, or whether the top little bit has gone up. I mean, it seems to me these are two different conversations, and the one we're having now is perfectly healthy, whereas the one on the top has something to it, and we want to look at that too, but it's not the same thing.*

A statistic I love, which came from Bob Fogel about 2004 or 2005, is that if you took the then poverty standard, which I don't remember what it was, and you looked at the population in the United States in the year 1900, 5 percent to 6 percent of Americans lived above the then poverty line. It's a great statistic, because the whole point is that what we've done very well is raise many incomes. We still have groups that aren't above the line. We still need growth and all the rest of it. But, please, let's distinguish between the two.

COCHRANE: That's what my point was. And I don't care how hedge-fund managers travel or how much money they have. Even if we make them all fly commercial and take all their money, we've got to fix this problem at the lower end. And to frame it as a solution to inequality, I think, is just a mistake.

OHANIAN: And I think that your point really highlights that economic growth's a wonderful thing, and so much of it comes from total factor productivity. Again, one thing that really disturbs me is the fact that business sector productivity, now for five years, has slowed from 2.5 percent to 0.9 percent. When you look at Europe, if you construct total factor productivity (TFP) using Penn World Tables data and using traditional one-third/two-thirds income shares, France, Italy, and Germany TFPs are either flat or lower today than they were in the late 1970s, which is shocking. Spanish TFP is down about 15 percent since the 1990s. Spanish TFP grew substantially from the 1970s up to about the early 1990s.

So I think that's a great question, because it brings back the idea of, "Economic growth can raise all boats." In some countries, you're not doing that. And productivity is the key. Some advanced countries are having a hard time and it looks like we might be entering that phase, based on the statistics that Steve and John have done. Maybe that's another topic for another conference.

CHAPTER EIGHT

Remembering Gary Becker

Dinner remarks by Edward P. Lazear and George P. Shultz

Part 1: Edward Lazear

This two-day conference celebrates Gary Becker's life. Although we rejoice in his many accomplishments, it is difficult to avoid being distracted by thoughts of what each of us has lost with Gary's passing. Of course, this is toughest for Guity and Gary's family, but we all share with them a deep feeling of emptiness.

Each of us who knew Gary personally has our own memories. For me, beyond the scholarly interaction that can never be replaced, there are little things that it is difficult to believe are gone: the many lovely dinners and casual lunches that we shared together; the frequent phone calls; the meetings in the office to chat about economics, politics, family, sports, and life in general; knowing that when things got tough or that when I needed advice, Gary would always be there. He was not only my dear friend and most important counselor, he was to me—as to many of us at Hoover and in the larger economics profession—an intellectual father.

Gary had a human side that I relished. I loved to tell Gary the latest joke and watch him laugh deeply. He teased me incessantly, most often making fun of the knowledge I lacked. "What?" Gary would say, only half-jokingly, "You never heard of so and so?" or "You mean you never read that?" and then he'd reference some obscure article or book.

Many of you knew Gary Becker through our Hoover family. You remember his brilliance at retreats, conferences, and other oral presentations. You recall his insightful op-eds and blogs. You know how important he was to our community as a thought leader. There is no doubt that Gary was—and will remain—among the most respected of Hoover scholars. In short, you remember Gary as a Hoover treasure.

But as each of us reflects on the personal aspects of our loss, it is easy to forget that Gary belonged not just to us, but to the world. Yes, Gary was a great economist, but beyond that, Gary was the person who advanced social science more than any other twentieth-century scholar. Gary's life was spent using his genius to understand issues in every realm of society. Gary wrote the seminal paper in seven literatures, most of which he started, and is one of the few economists who deserved to win multiple Nobel prizes.

Gary was enormously creative, but as much as that, he had intellectual courage. Gary's work was not only revolutionary, it was viewed by many to be heresy. How dare an economist talk about such important moral dilemmas as discrimination in cost-benefit terms? Who in his right mind would think of a child as a consumer durable?

In the early years, one illustrious economist, when asked about Gary's work, replied, "Yes, I read Gary Becker. I enjoy American humor."

But Gary persisted. Even though he was a very young man and was going down a path that could be disastrous for his career, he believed that what he was doing would truly help us understand the world. He had confidence in his work and the catcalls from his detractors would not deter him.

Gary won. He not only silenced his critics, he turned many of them into followers as they came to understand the power of his reasoning, logic, and innovation. His analysis was not only the most innovative, it was the truth.

A powerful example comes to mind. One of my Stanford Business School colleague's wife was writing on women and the family and my colleague suggested that she read Gary's transformational *Treatise on the Family*. She was anti-economics, anti-Chicago, and anti-Becker, but she read the book. After reading it, she was awestruck. Her reaction was that the work was brilliant, thoughtful, and dedicated. It was, she thought, the epitome of serious intellectual reasoning and reflected, more than anything, a desire to truly understand this important subject.

The pursuit of scientific knowledge and truth was Gary's hallmark. We all know how much Gary believed in economics. Economics was not a game to be played to satisfy intellectual curiosity or to win academic chess-matches. Economics was the most powerful tool a scholar could have for understanding social phenomena. Gary once said that he used to think that economics could be used to explain all human behavior, but that he had changed his view. He now thought that economics could explain all behavior, human and non-human alike.

Gary's first major work was his doctoral dissertation on the economics of discrimination. Gary's goal was to understand how discrimination would affect the well-being of those who were the victims of discrimination and when discrimination's effects would be most pernicious. Gary reasoned that disfavored individuals worked first for those firms that had the least distaste for them, which implied that when there were large numbers of people in the disfavored group, the wages of that group would be much below that of the favored group because they would be forced to work even for those who had strong distastes for their kind. Thus, for example, African Americans as a large group suffer more from discrimination than Jews, who are a much smaller group, even when comparing individuals with the same education and skills. This proposition and the many others that are implied by the theory have been verified empirically.

Around 1960, Becker puzzled over why consumption patterns among various groups differed. Why, for example, do the rich play golf and the poor play basketball? Why do the rich attend opera and the poor watch TV? Is it possible to simply assume the answer, postulating that the rich have different tastes than the poor? Gary was not satisfied with such simple tautologies. Instead, he reasoned that sports, like all "commodities," required two inputs: goods and time. Individuals who have high wages have a high value of time, which makes the time component more expensive to them than to those with lower wages. High-wage CEOs cannot afford to take much time off because the value of their time at work is so high. As a result, the rich tend to produce entertainment using a larger share of goods and the poor use a larger share of time. Opera is "goods intensive," with high ticket prices. Watching TV is "time intensive," requiring little in the way of expenditure on goods. Rather than resorting to ethnic or racial explanations or stereotypes, Gary's theory implied that the poor play basketball because it requires much time but little in the way of goods, whereas the rich combine their high-priced time with much more expensive goods inputs like golf fees.

Another of Gary's most important policy implications came from his economic theory of fertility. Gary observed that in the nineteenth century, high-income families were larger than low-income families, but in the latter part of the twentieth century, the pattern was reversed with the poor having the largest families. Gary reasoned that raising a child combined both goods and time, primarily time of the mother. The time cost varied with the mother's wage rate. The "cost of a child" was lower to low-wage women because the value of their time in the labor market was lower than that of a high-wage woman. As a result, he postulated that families where the mother has low wages are likely to be larger than families with high-wage mothers. This implication is found to be true almost universally. Today, immigrant families with low-wage women are large, whereas the families of professional women are small. Female professionals have fewer children because they cannot "afford" to take time off to raise a large number of children, not because they love children less than their poorer counterparts. The cost of taking time off work is higher for professional women than for low-wage women and, as a result, they work more and spend less time in the home raising children. In the nineteenth century, the pattern was the reverse because women with rich husbands did not work and the value of their time outside the home was low.

This theory not only has been verified time and time again, but it gave the prescription that the most effective way to reduce population growth is to educate girls so that they will have high wages in adulthood, which induces them to have fewer children. This policy has become a widely accepted part of economic development.

The theory of human capital was developed most forcefully by Becker in the 1960s. He argued that human capital was most commonly obtained through formal schooling and through learning on the job. The theory yielded very specific predictions for education and wage patterns over the work life. The educational establishment was at first hostile to this view, thinking that treating education as a mere income-producer belittled education and those engaged in it. That view changed as the evidence mounted that the single most important factor in raising income was education. This not only illustrated the importance and relevance of the theory, but made education and teachers all the more important to society.

Gary's *Treatise on the Family* was a comprehensive view of much that went on in family life, again using the tools of economics to reason through behavior in an ultra-rational fashion. He understood caring for children not only as an act of love, but also as an investment. He studied gifts, bequests, and primogenitor (giving all of an estate to the first born). He examined family formation and its dissolution in the context of human capital. For example, his theories of marriage and divorce reasoned that those who had more "family specific capital" were more likely to stay together, which is why families with children have lower divorce rates than those without, why divorce rates fall with years of marriage, and why couples who are well-matched in education levels, religion, and other characteristics are more likely to stay together. Becker's family economics was, like his other theories, resisted at the outset. Its empirical predictions that were borne out in so many different environments convinced most of his critics to the extent that it is now thought of as mainstream. The best evidence of its universality is that Gary was awarded the Nobel Prize in large part for his work on the family.

There are many other areas in which Gary made seminal contributions. These include understanding the trade-off between punishment and crime detection as deterrents to crime, how advertising affects consumer preferences, and how to provide organs for transplants in the most efficient way. The list goes on.

Despite Gary's love of scholarship, he was a devoted family man who not only loved his children and grandchildren, but appreciated them enormously. He often spoke of how fortunate he was to have Guity as his wife.

The fact that he was devoted to his family did not prevent him from devoting time and effort to others, most notably his colleagues and students. Many of us, I among them, went to the University of Chicago to be with Gary. Gary was my idol, even as I obtained my PhD among the infidels at Harvard. Being able to come to Chicago as an assistant professor was a dream come true. That's because Gary made us all better. Sitting in workshops with him, watching him think, listening to his comments, and being the victim of his criticism were invaluable to our intellectual development. There is no better way to become a good economist than to be an assistant professor under Gary Becker.

All of us here know that Gary's powers of concentration were truly exceptional. Even at eighty-three, Gary was always attentive to the topic being discussed. While people forty years his junior were dozing in seminars, Gary was always alert, intense, and involved. Gary loved research and he loved the academic life, which consists mostly of proposing and shooting down new ideas. In his last days, Guity told me how his doctors were amazed at his awareness and power to reason, even when his body was so weak. I responded that I wasn't surprised at all. Gary had so much practice staying focused in thousands of boring seminars that he could outwit anyone, no matter what his physical condition. He never gave up on thinking critically. He maintained his love for doing research until his last day.

We all knew that Gary would die with his boots on, and he did so, galloping faster than the rest of us. A couple of months ago, Gary co-authored and presented a paper entitled "The Manipulation of Children's Preferences, Old Age Support, and Investment in Children's Human Capital," at a conference here at Stanford. It was unbelievable. Here was an octogenarian presenting a high-quality paper that reminded me of work that he was capable of doing fifty years earlier. All the conference participants and my Stanford colleagues remarked at how impressive he was, how much energy and clarity he had. Indeed, it is true. Gary was youthful until his last day.

Gary Becker was an intellectual giant. He was the kind of person who comes along only a few times each century. For this reason, we are overwhelmed by the enormity of our loss. But it is more important to remember how much we all gained from having Gary with us for over eight decades. As we celebrate his life, let us be grateful for the riches that Gary bestowed on his friends and family and for the immense positive impact that he had on scholarship, on policy, and on humankind.

Part 2: George Shultz

Thank you, Eddie, for that terrific exposition about Gary and his work. I learned a lot by listening to you, but not as much as I learned by listening to Gary when he was around here.

This is a conference about inequality, and somehow the topic is appropriate, but I also think we should recognize that Gary was the epitome of inequality. He was so gifted, so different, so superior, that you had to shake your head and say, "I've got to listen to that guy. He has something really important to say."

You also recognize that high quality has many dimensions. Gary reminded me once of a little scene in one of Milton Friedman's *Free to Choose* videos. Milton has his nose pressed up against the glass as he watches a young girl playing a violin, and he says to himself, "I wish I were that talented." So talent has many dimensions.

I thought I'd give you a few reminiscences of our time together. First of all, there is the Chicago-Hoover connection. I had the great privilege of being at the University of Chicago for quite a while and participating in that intense intellectual atmosphere. Gary was there in economics, as was Milton. George Stigler's office was right across the hall from mine. So I got to know George and Milton and Gary very well in that setting.

Then, of course, out here at Hoover, here they were again: Milton, George, Gary. There's a wonderful picture of them that Guity gave me today. Isn't that terrific? Those were three giants. They respected each other, they listened to each other, they argued with each other, and it was just sensational. So I'm wearing a coat that has both Stanford and University of Chicago colors.

I used to organize what we called an economists' weekend every year. Bechtel has a wonderful place called Villa Cypress near Carmel, and when I was associated with Bechtel, we would go down there. George, Milton, Gary, and Walt Wriston were usually there. Walt was the smartest banker that ever existed. We would have

George Stigler, Milton Friedman, and Gary Becker (from left to right).

extended conversations. We'd arrive on Friday afternoon and have a continuous conversation until we left on Sunday afternoon, and it was really stimulating. Usually Gary would drive Milton down, and by the time they got there, they were just steamed up and ready to talk.

I was always amazed at the practicality of these people. When I was in office, they were sort of my unpaid casual consultants, because I'd call up Gary or Milton or George and relate a problem. They would always have good ideas that were practical, usable—not just theory.

A few months ago I had the occasion of writing an op-ed with Gary. That was really an experience. We talked about our subject, we found we agreed, and then we started to pin it down a little more clearly. Then we put our ideas into writing and I was really impressed with Gary's care with words, his insistence that our piece would be absolutely clear, with no ambiguity—no "on this hand or the other hand." Our op-ed was on a revenue-neutral carbon tax and how it was important to be sure we had a system for being sure that it was revenue neutral—no ifs, ands, or buts about it. That was quite a good experience.

What these people and Gary insisted on was getting factual content to go with ideas. Ideas were important, but if an idea couldn't be tested with the reality of empirical research—with facts—well, it wasn't worth much. He had this connection between ideas and facts. Milton had the same characteristic, and I sang this song at his ninetieth birthday, but it also applies to Gary. It goes like this:

A fact without a theory is like a kite without a tail,

Is like a boat without a rudder,

Is like a ship without a sail.

A fact without a theory is sad as sad can be,

But if there's one thing worse in this universe,

It's a theory . . . I said a theory . . . I mean a theory without a fact!

Conference on Inequality in Memory of Gary Becker

September 25–26, 2014

Stauffer Auditorium
Hoover Institution, Stanford University

This conference is in memory of Gary Becker and will explore various measures of inequality and pose the question whether or not it is increasing. In exploring this question and examining policy implications, presenters will draw, where possible, on research on human capital and intergenerational mobility. Presenters will address the key policy question of what to do, with particular attention during the discussion to those at the bottom of the income distribution and the overall effects on economic growth.

Thursday, September 25

11:30 AM   **Registration and Lunch**

12:30 PM   **Welcome**
John Raisian, Hoover Institution
John B. Taylor, Hoover Institution and
Stanford University

12:45 PM   **Introductory Remarks**
James Pierson

1:30 PM   ***The Effects of Redistribution Policies on Growth
and Employment***
Casey B. Mulligan, University of Chicago

2:30 PM   **Break**

2:45 PM   ***The Broad-Based Rise in the Return to Top Talent***
            Joshua D. Rauh, Hoover Institution and
            Stanford University

3:45 PM   ***The Economic Determinants of Top Income Inequality***
            Charles I. Jones, Stanford University

4:45 PM   **Adjourn**

6:30 PM   **Reception on the Exhibit Pavilion Patio**

7:00 PM   **Dinner in the Hoover Tower Lawn Tent with
            Dinner Remarks**
            Edward P. Lazear, Hoover Institution and
            Stanford University
            George P. Shultz, Hoover Institution

Friday, September 26

8:00 AM   **Continental Breakfast**

8:30 AM   ***Intergenerational Mobility and Income Inequality:
            Facts, Explanations, and Policy Implications***
            Jörg Spenkuch, Northwestern University

9:15 AM   ***Income and Wealth Inequality in America and Policies
            to Address It***
            Kevin M. Murphy, University of Chicago
            Emmanuel Saez, University of California, Berkeley

10:30 PM   **Concluding Panel on Solutions**
            Panelists: John H. Cochrane, University of Chicago
                     Lee E. Ohanian, UCLA
                     George P. Shultz, Hoover Institution

12:00 PM   **Adjourn and Lunch**

About the Contributors

TOM CHURCH is a research fellow at the Hoover Institution. He studies income inequality, poverty, health care policy, entitlement reform, and immigration reform. He has conducted research on developing supplemental statistics to better measure income, poverty, and health insurance coverage in the United States. He also contributes to the Hoover Institution's immigration reform initiative. He received his master's degree in public policy with honors from Pepperdine University, specializing in economics and international relations.

JOHN H. COCHRANE is the AQR Capital Management Distinguished Service Professor of Finance at the University of Chicago's Booth School of Business, a senior fellow at the Hoover Institution, a research associate of the National Bureau of Economic Research, and an adjunct scholar of the Cato Institute. His academic publications focus on finance, macroeconomics, and monetary economics, with forays into health insurance and time-series econometrics. He also writes op-eds for the *Wall Street Journal* and blogs as *The Grumpy Economist.*

CHARLES I. JONES is the STANCO 25 Professor of Economics at the Stanford Graduate School of Business and a research associate of the National Bureau of Economic Research. He has been honored as a national fellow at the Hoover Institution, a John M. Olin Foundation faculty fellow, and an Alfred P. Sloan Foundation research fellow. His research has been supported by a series of grants from the National Science Foundation. He is the author of numerous research papers as well as two textbooks, *Introduction to Economic Growth* (2013) and *Macroeconomics* (2014).

EDWARD P. LAZEAR is the Morris Arnold and Nona Jean Cox Senior Fellow at the Hoover Institution and the Jack Steele Parker Professor of

Human Resources, Management and Economics at Stanford University's Graduate School of Business. He served at the White House from 2006 to 2009, where he was chairman of the President's Council of Economic Advisers. Before coming to Stanford, he taught at the University of Chicago. He has written or edited a dozen books and has published more than one hundred papers in leading professional journals

CHRISTOPHER MILLER is the associate director of the Program in Grand Strategy at Yale University as well as a fellow at the Foreign Policy Research Institute in Philadelphia. He recently finished a book, *Collapse: The Struggle to Save the Soviet Economy,* and is currently writing *Putinomics: The Price of Power in Russia.* Miller's other research interests include political economy, economic history, and financial history. He has served as a research fellow at Stanford's Hoover Institution, a research associate at the Brookings Institution, and a lecturer at the New Economic School in Moscow. He received his doctorate from Yale University and his bachelor's degree from Harvard.

CASEY B. MULLIGAN, a professor of economics at the University of Chicago, has served as a visiting professor teaching public economics at Harvard University, Clemson University, and the Irving B. Harris Graduate School of Public Policy Studies at the University of Chicago. He is affiliated with the National Bureau of Economic Research, the George J. Stigler Center for the Study of the Economy and the State, and the Population Research Center. His research covers capital and labor taxation, the gender wage gap, health economics, Social Security, voting, and the economics of aging.

KEVIN M. MURPHY is the George J. Stigler Distinguished Service Professor of Economics in the Booth School of Business and the Department of Economics at the University of Chicago. He is a senior fellow at the Hoover Institution, a fellow of the Econometric Society, an elected member of the American Academy of Arts and Sciences, and a MacArthur fellow. He won the John Bates Clark Medal in 1997 for his work on wage inequality and unemployment.

LEE E. OHANIAN is a senior fellow at the Hoover Institution and a professor of economics and director of the Ettinger Family Program in Macroeconomic Research at UCLA. His research focuses on economic crises, technological change and inequality, and the impact of taxation on economic activity. He is an adviser to the Federal Reserve Bank of Minneapolis and has previously advised other federal reserve banks. He previously served on the faculties of the Universities of Minnesota and Pennsylvania. He is co-director of the research initiative Macroeconomics across Time and Space at the National Bureau of Economic Research.

JAMES PIERESON is president of the William E. Simon Foundation and a senior fellow at the Manhattan Institute. He is a frequent contributor to various journals and newspapers, including *Commentary, New Criterion, American Political Science Review, Public Interest, Philanthropy, American Spectator, Wall Street Journal, Weekly Standard, National Review,* and *Washington Post.* He is also the author of *Camelot and the Cultural Revolution: How the Assassination of John F. Kennedy Shattered American Liberalism.*

JOSHUA D. RAUH is a senior fellow at the Hoover Institution and a professor of finance at the Stanford Graduate School of Business. He formerly taught at the University of Chicago's Booth School of Business (2004–09) and the Kellogg School of Management (2009–12). His research covers a range of topics, including corporate investment and financial structure, public pension liabilities, and the determinants of the distribution of household incomes. His research has received national media coverage in outlets such as the *Wall Street Journal,* the *New York Times,* the *Financial Times,* and *The Economist.*

EMMANUEL SAEZ is a professor of economics and director of the Center for Equitable Growth at the University of California, Berkeley. His research focuses on tax policy and inequality from both theoretical and empirical perspectives. Jointly with Thomas Piketty, he has constructed long-run historical series of income inequality in the United States that have been widely discussed in the public debate. He was awarded the John Bates Clark medal of the American Economic Association in 2009 and a MacArthur Fellowship in 2010.

GEORGE P. SHULTZ is the Thomas W. and Susan B. Ford Distinguished Fellow at the Hoover Institution. He served as secretary of labor (1969–70); director, Office of Management and Budget (1970–72); secretary of the Treasury (1972–74); and secretary of state (1982–89). In 1989, he became the Jack Steele Parker Professor of International Economics at the Stanford Graduate School of Business and a distinguished fellow at the Hoover Institution. He is the Advisory Council chair of Stanford's Precourt Institute for Energy Efficiency, chair of the MIT Energy Initiative External Advisory Board, and chair of the Hoover Institution Task Force on Energy Policy.

JÖRG L. SPENKUCH is an assistant professor of managerial economics and decision sciences at Northwestern University's Kellogg School of Management. He joined the Kellogg faculty in 2013 after receiving his doctorate from the University of Chicago, where he studied under the supervision of Gary Becker and Steven Levitt. His research interests include political economy, labor economics, and applied microeconomics more generally. He is currently working on issues related to inequality, strategic behavior in nonmarket environments, and the interaction between religion and political extremism.

JOHN B. TAYLOR is the Mary and Robert Raymond Professor of Economics at Stanford University and the George P. Shultz Senior Fellow in Economics at Stanford's Hoover Institution. He is also the director of Stanford's Introductory Economics Center. He has served on the President's Council of Economic Advisers and as undersecretary of the treasury for international affairs. He received the Alexander Hamilton Award and the Treasury Distinguished Service Award for his policy contributions at the US Treasury and the Medal of the Republic of Uruguay for his work in resolving its 2002 financial crisis.

About the Hoover Institution's
Working Group on Economic Policy

The Working Group on Economic Policy brings together experts on economic and financial policy at the Hoover Institution to study key developments in the US and global economies, examine their interactions, and develop specific policy proposals.

For twenty-five years starting in the early 1980s, the United States economy experienced an unprecedented economic boom. Economic expansions were stronger and longer than in the past. Recessions were shorter, shallower, and less frequent. GDP doubled and household net worth increased by 250 percent in real terms. Forty-seven million jobs were created.

This quarter-century boom strengthened as its length increased. Productivity growth surged by one full percentage point per year in the United States, creating an additional $9 trillion of goods and services that would never have existed. And the long boom went global with emerging market countries from Asia to Latin America to Africa experiencing the enormous improvements in both economic growth and economic stability.

Economic policies that place greater reliance on the principles of free markets, price stability, and flexibility have been the key to these successes. Recently, however, several powerful new economic forces have begun to change the economic landscape, and these principles are being challenged with far reaching implications for US economic policy, both domestic and international. A financial crisis flared up in 2007 and turned into a severe panic in 2008 leading to the Great Recession. How we interpret and react to these forces—and in particular whether proven policy principles prevail going forward—will determine whether strong economic growth and stability returns and again continues to spread and improve more people's lives or whether the economy stalls and stagnates.

Our Working Group organizes seminars and conferences, prepares policy papers and other publications, and serves as a resource for policymakers and interested members of the public.

Inequality and Economic Policy: Essays in Honor of Gary Becker
Edited by Tom Church, Chris Miller, and John B. Taylor

Making Failure Feasible: How Bankruptcy Reform Can End "Too Big to Fail"*
Edited by Kenneth E. Scott, Thomas H. Jackson, and John B. Taylor

Across the Great Divide: New Perspectives on the Financial Crisis
Edited by Martin Neil Baily and John B. Taylor

Bankruptcy Not Bailout: A Special Chapter 14*
Edited by Kenneth E. Scott and John B. Taylor

Government Policies and the Delayed Economic Recovery
Edited by Lee E. Ohanian, John B. Taylor, and Ian J. Wright

Why Capitalism?
Allan H. Meltzer

First Principles: Five Keys to Restoring America's Prosperity
John B. Taylor

Ending Government Bailouts as We Know Them*
Edited by Kenneth E. Scott, George P. Shultz, and John B. Taylor

How Big Banks Fail: And What to Do about It*
Darrell Duffie

The Squam Lake Report: Fixing the Financial System
Darrell Duffie et al.

Getting Off Track: How Government Actions and Interventions Caused, Prolonged, and Worsened the Financial Crisis
John B. Taylor

The Road Ahead for the Fed
Edited by John B. Taylor and John D. Ciorciari

Putting Our House in Order: A Guide to Social Security and Health Care Reform
George P. Shultz and John B. Shoven

Index